W9-BHZ-736

THE DOLL

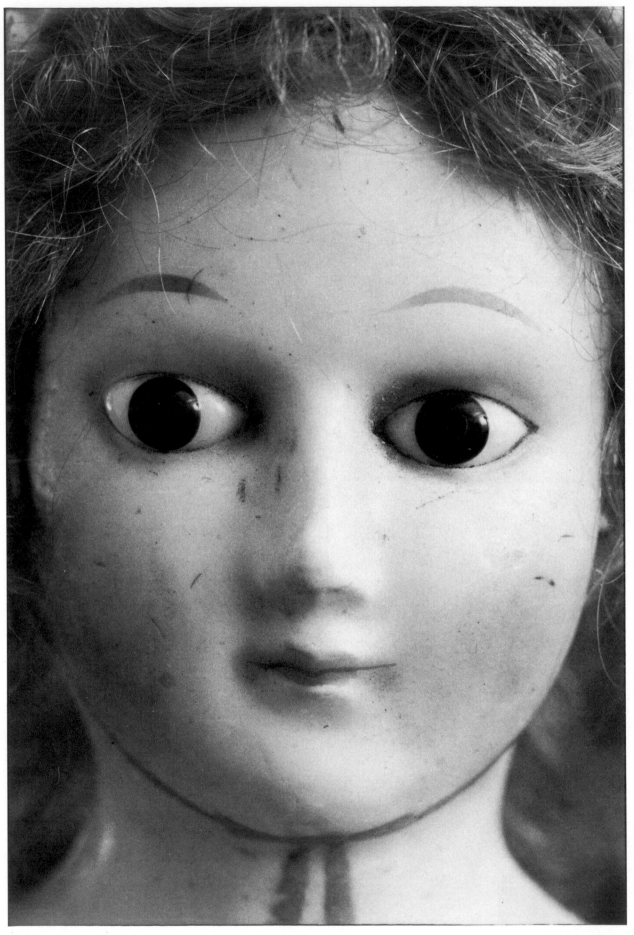

PLATE I

NEW SHORTER EDITION

THE DOLL

TEXT BY
CARL FOX

PHOTOGRAPHS BY
H. LANDSHOFF

HARRY N. ABRAMS, INC., PUBLISHERS, NEW YORK

DISTRIBUTED BY NEW AMERICAN LIBRARY

FOR ROSE

(on preceding page)

1. Is this wide-eyed innocence, or rather the sudden
knowledge thrust upon Eve when "the eyes of them
both were opened, and they knew they were naked; and
they sewed fig leaves together, and made themselves
aprons." What might not have been noticed in the
complete doll has been brought to our attention by the
photographer's awareness in this sensitively lighted
close-up of a wax-over-composition doll, with mohair
wig and brown, pupilless glass eyes, made in Germany about 1830–40. *Collection Margaret Whitton,
Bridgewater, Conn.*

Library of Congress Cataloging in Publication Data

Fox, Carl, 1913–
  The doll.

  Bibliography: p.
    1. Dolls. I. Landshoff, H., illus. II. Title.
NK4893.F69   1973   745.59'22   73-8529

Library of Congress Catalogue Card Number: 73-8529
All rights reserved. No part of the contents of this book
may be reproduced without the written permission of the publishers
HARRY N. ABRAMS, INC., New York
Printed and bound in Japan

CONTENTS

ACKNOWLEDGEMENTS

Without the enthusiastic assistance of the doll collectors I would not have enjoyed the dual pleasure of meeting them and their lovely companions. To them and collectors everywhere, I gratefully dedicate this book. Particular thanks are owed to those persons listed below who gave so much of their knowledge and their time. (Mistakes are mine alone.)

Bart Anderson, Mary Anne McLean Bradford, Irving Chais, Miss Elizabeth Ann Coleman, Mrs. Marjorie Merritt Darrah, Mrs. Betsy Distler, Frederick J. Dockstader, Ernest S. Dodge, Mrs. Irene Dodge, Mrs. Elizabeth M. Donoghue, Grace Dyar, André Emmerich, Miss Mariellen Fox, Mrs. Rose Fox, Miss June Henneberger, Mr. and Mrs. Irwin Hersey, James J. Hesline, Thomas Kyle, Mrs. Ursula Landshoff, Martin Leifer, David Little, Jay-Ehret Mahoney, Ruth E. and R. C. Mathes, Mrs. Mary Merritt, Gene Moore, Mrs. Margaret Patterson, Mr. and Mrs. Leo Rabkin, Mrs. Dorrie Reedy, Mr. and Mrs. Louis F. Simon, Nathaniel Spear, Jr., William Steig, the Trustees of the Margaret Woodbury Strong Museum of Fascination, Miss Frances Walker, and Mrs. Margaret Whitton.

INTRODUCTION

Visual satisfaction cannot be explained, although millions of words have been expended in the attempt. I will not add to them except to point out that the photographs that follow are a series of visual mountain peaks which may excite your admiration, wonder, and "enchantment of the heart."[1] These peaks are not to be climbed to the summit; those unapproachable last few yards will always remain—which is just as it should be, for a work of art or a mountain peak. It is the difference between satiety and mystery. The full, open-eyed stare of the doll makes a portrait no less enigmatic than the painting of the brooding *Ginevra de' Benci* in the National Gallery of Art in Washington, D. C.,[2] even though this is not to suggest a comparable mastery.

Since portrait painting and portrait sculpture are out of fashion, it is with some relief that we can indulge our taste for the timeless beauty of the human face, however it is depicted. We believe that the portrait painter's unique contribution of catching a likeness, both physical and spiritual, is similar to that of the doll maker, and that the latter's art of multiplication may be as pertinent as the mass-produced color reproductions of an original painting. Dolls are no more impersonal than any portrait in stone, ceramic, bronze, or wood.

Fashions and fashionable painters have played their adult version of leapfrog over and over, recalling the central figures in the painting *Children's Games* by Pieter Bruegel the Elder.[3] Of course, Bruegel's pictures tell stories. The child in Everyman insists that his pictures have stories and his stories have pictures, whether or not they are sensible. Haven't our favorite stories and poems often combined the apparently logical with large doses of the absurd? Over the years I have followed the adventures of Edward Lear's Violet, Slingsby, Guy, and Lionel, appropriately illustrated by the drawing master to Queen Victoria, who concludes his tale: "As for the Rhinoceros, in token of their grateful adherence, they had him killed and stuffed directly, and then set him up outside the door of their father's house as a diaphanous doorscraper."[4] Bruegel and Lear told the truth as they saw it. I believe that they looked truth in the eye and saw through it to their own vision of the world beyond, to that landscape of the inner eye that transcends reality.

So would I persuade you to follow our erratic wanderings in a Bruegelian landscape of dolls. The composition of our picture story reflects the world of the camera, dependent on light and governed in its use thereof by the insights of the photographer. Of the nine hundred and ninety-nine ways of looking at a doll[5] he chose his own, which for him was the only way, the way of the artist searching for the truth within his point of view. Shift the angle of vision and the light source a little to the left or right, up or down, and other faces and other stories rise to the surface. The marriage of enthusiasm (mine) with professionalism (his) has not taken us quite round the world in search of "The Doll"; but within the smaller compass of several states along the eastern seaboard of the United States we have surveyed upwards of forty thousand dolls. A mere introduction to the number not seen. Those are the ones that will forever continue to haunt us. Why, you will ask, has *she* been included and not so-and-so, whom everyone knows to be superior, rarer, indeed, the only example of her kind in the world? Because, in essence, this has been a personal odyssey, restricted by our limitations of knowledge and time. More than anything else, this selection is the narrative of a voyage of discovery.

The path of our search, which had been circuitous and often repetitive, inasmuch as most of the dolls seen were classic chinas, bisques, and woodens, suddenly was redirected on our seeing the museum collections in Salem. Our delight was reaffirmed by the knowledge that many of these dolls were brought home there by the merchants and sea captains of the eighteenth and nineteenth centuries. The world in miniature had been made real, and no longer was the pride of collecting confined to what I had begun to think of as a "chastity of dolls." The New England scene revealed a clear-eyed honesty about the world at large and a full perception of that world in particular, even in its playthings.[6]

Now the collector began to take shape behind the collections. The doll maker in this instance was a certain Mrs. Lucy Hiller Cleveland, whose dolls include a jubilant slave with a cat-o'-nine-tails captive in one sling-supported arm while the other holds aloft a paper printed with the single word FREE. His wrinkled leather face is split by a smile of unalloyed happiness. Another of Mrs. Cleveland's dolls, her Turkish Delight, seems to take on the appearance of an itinerant vagabond who she decided was the very model of a pipe-smoking, sybaritic (he sits cross-legged on a huge pillow) Turk. One does not quite believe in his Turkishness, but he is familiar as the unshaven peddler or cadging tramp at her kitchen door. There is humor and compassion in her small world. As a primitive painter Mrs. Cleveland might have enriched our collection of Americana; as a maker of dolls, her modest place in American art remains quietly secure in the case devoted to her creations at the Essex Institute in Salem. Certainly her figure of Freedom is a rare statement of the Puritan conscience. Our excuse for not including her dolls in our book may be considered no excuse at all—they were not photogenic. In no way does this negate their quality. Many of the dolls we photographed were not cooperative, and their temperament, which I understand and accept, compelled us to discard a great many photographs, thereby establishing yet another kind of Salon des Refusés!

The people and places we visited have not all been described. They stand confidently in the background, the guardians of treasures that will survive long after this voyage is documented and filed away. Our debt to them can be repaid only in the tender loving care we give their possessions. Our search through cabinets of dolls, looking for we-knew-not-what, our being stopped short, gripped by a fugitive smile, a chipped nose, a madness in the eyes— these are intangibles not given to classification. My trade, and it is arguable that such a trade exists, is judgment.

Judgments are peculiarly evasive when they are concerned with beauty, taste, and the eccentricity of individual reactions to objects, people, and places. The antidote, of course, is a contrary judgment. My reactions are opinionated and oblique, as are my associations to poetic and other memories which the dolls have evoked. One might say that it is by our associations that we should be judged. This collection is an exhibition, and "every exhibition is, or should be, an attempt at developing man's qualities and a pleasure to the eye. Technically speaking it is a composition whose elements are the shape and material of the objects, the play of colours and light . . . and a certain striving after poetic overtones which should, as with any genuine work of art, work the miracle of transmitting the emotions of life through inanimate things."[7]

We offer you a gallery of doll portraits drawn in time, place, and cultural history. They are images of mankind that confront you with unblinking eyes, wherein you may find the mirror of beauty, memory, and childhood grace.[8] The reflections are multiple, pleasant, and even perverse. What we strive for is a talisman for memories, a conjuration to evoke for you some feeling of innocence, delight, and mystery. Perhaps the greatest single attraction of the doll is its almost magical power to engulf the viewer and lift him out of himself into the doll's world—whatever it may be.

CARL FOX

11

THE DOLL

Experts rarely agree. It is their inalienable right to provoke, to stir up, and to incite to disagreement. The game should be played with skill, devotion, and a stubbornness associated with anchorites. Playthings and games may be almost anything,[9] and their definitions are just as flexible, for they depend on what one wishes to accept or reject. It is not easy to cleanse the mind of decades of restricting varnish. How many layers must be removed, and without damage to the original? When I joined the game I began with what I believed was a simple question. I expected a simple answer to "What is a doll?"

I turned to my reference shelf. Webster's says that a doll is "a children's toy made to resemble a baby, child, or grown person." That is an uncluttered definition with which one should not quarrel. However, it does not satisfy me. It leaves the windows of the mind wide open, but most of us looking out the windows at a baby, child, or grown person cannot see the doll beneath the walking, talking figures. In brief, Webster's is poor fare for anyone seeking doll expertise. There is, however, a learned work long treasured by students and a certain group of peripatetic salesmen. The *Encyclopaedia Britannica* (1945) stands aloof and sober in the confusion of my bookshelves. "The doll, the familiar toy puppet of childhood, is one of the oldest of human institutions." Revealed are two additional facts: puppet and institution. I have my own ideas and mind pictures of both, and neither seems to encourage me nor to placate the rising irritation born of my sense of frustration. The irritation was at my own inadequacy. I did not understand. Once more I turned to *Webster's New World Dictionary of the American Language*. Because it is important and germane to our investigation I will not expurgate: "pup·pet (pup′it), *n.* [ME. *popet;* OFr. *poupette*, dim.<LL. **puppa*<L. *pupa*, a girl, doll, puppet], 1. a small figure that is a likeness of the human form; doll. 2. such a figure moved by attached strings or wires, or by the hands, in a puppet show. 3. a person whose actions, ideas, etc. are controlled by another."

My confidence in authority[10] suffered a final blow when I picked up the distinguished *Shorter Oxford English Dictionary* and read: "Doll . . . 1. A female pet, a mistress. 2. A girl's toy-baby. 3. A pretty but silly woman." I was prompted to banish all of them with the most damning, unequivocal word I could find in their pages—nonsense: "1. words or actions that convey an absurd meaning or no meaning at all."

A birthday book I purchased for myself, written by one of the great contemporary masters and historians of puppetry, Bil Baird,[11] was found and consulted. He declares that "a puppet is an inanimate figure that is made to move by human effort before an audience. . . .

It is definitely not a doll" (italics mine). Here is an authority who does not mince words. He is an expert who has devoted his life to expanding his skills and knowledge. He has discovered and collected puppets old and new. Most important, he is a vital, creative force, anything but a textbook, a dictionary, or an encyclopedia. Conversely: a doll is definitely not a puppet.[12] Yes and no.

The late Ralph Altman wrote: "It is not always apparent whether a given sculptured effigy ought to be classified as puppet or doll, as component of a mask or simply as a statuette. Its function might be unknown, like that of the articulated clay figurines from prehistoric Mexico; or it might have multiple functions such as certain statuettes which were manipulated as sacred instruments of divination in several parts of the world, including ancient Egypt."[13]

An innocent inquiry had led to depths I had never dreamed of exploring. What is a doll if not a plaything, a toy[14] or a puppet? And whose definitions are we to believe? Undoubtedly there were images made as "objects of ritualistic and sacred import."[15] Is man the artificer really concerned about what we label his creations? Image or doll or puppet? My unanswered questions hovered round my head like twittering birds. As Victor Hugo cogently observed: "In the same way as birds make a nest of anything, children make a doll of no matter what." Yes, and how applicable to my understanding of children and playthings.

Adult perceptions of childhood are limited by a storehouse of good and bad memories. The damaged memory is buried in the gloom of storage bins[16] and bears a label reading: NOT TO BE REMOVED OR DISTURBED. The absence of these damaged memories forces us to reconstruct childhood with an incomplete set of building blocks. How one envies the memory of an author or friend who seems to recall everything! But how much is truth and how much fiction? Did I play with dolls? Yes, paper dolls that I cut from the family magazines, dressed and undressed, and then discarded with each issue. I believe I recall the difficulty of manipulating the scissors, and the awkwardness with which I rounded the corners or ruined the tiny paper tabs. Did I play with dolls? An early and fond memory of a doll (toy) concerns my Teddy Bear. I hugged him, I beat him, I slept with him, and one day I pulled out his button eyes. But Teddy Bear is not a representation of a human being and therefore cannot be called a doll. Or can he? A friendly devil's advocate from New England, professor of English and father of three children, spoke of his children's Teddy Bear as "doll and playmate." His question "Where do you draw the line?" confounded me. All I could think of was Humpty-Dumpty's reply to Alice: "When *I* use a word . . . it means just what I choose it to mean— neither more nor less."[17] This pronouncement is in no way different from William Empson's: "I claimed at the start that I would use the term 'ambiguity' to mean anything I liked."[18] Whether one is a scientific Frankenstein, a Pygmalion who imbues his statue of Galatea with life, or, as is familiar to the theatergoer of our time, a Professor Higgins who creates a "lady" from a "guttersnipe," the intent is the same—the transformation of a human shape into the stuff of dreams. Men would be like gods and animate the inanimate to create their illusions of reality. Prehistoric man worked in clay, and his three-dimensional figures were talismans of fertility. All objects were religious and magical, performing good and evil as projected by the worshiper, the priest, or the witch doctor. Belief was omnipresent. How could it have been otherwise in a hostile world? Man's sophisticated technical achievements had not yet supplanted his covert fears.

On Monday, September 15, 1969, this reader of the *New York Times* was caught by the headline "Where Religion and Superstition Mix in the City."[19] It was a lengthy article, accompanied by a photograph of some shelves of religious figures and various labeled bottles; an elderly white-haired man was shown standing behind his counter. The caption read: "Alberto Rendon, owner of Rendon's West Indies Botanical Garden in East Harlem, sells variety of perfumes, salts and incense. He says they bring 'peace and tranquility.'" The article continued:

The blending of Christianity and superstition has produced a flourishing business for "botanicas" [*sic*] (Spanish for botany)—stores that at one time sold only herbs but that today do a thriving business in amulets, statuary, perfumes and candles. . . . They cater to Puerto Rican, West Indian, Cuban, Dominican and other believers in "espiritismo," or spiritism, which holds that spirits summoned from another world have a direct effect—for good or evil.

Its roots are deep in the religions and beliefs of the African slaves who were brought to the New World, as well as in the practices of the Indians and Spanish and French colonists in the Caribbean.

Practitioners of spiritism say there is great similarity between their beliefs and those of the traditional religions. They point to angels, devils, saints and holy spirits as manifestations of the spirit world. . . .

"Our beliefs are not different," said Carmelo Ramos, who operates a botanica. . . . "We are just traveling different roads to reach the same goal."

While Mr. Ramos prefers to cater to persons who are seeking the help of "good" spirits, he does not turn away those who seek to cast spells or to delve into "black magic." For them he has vials of "bats' blood," "snake oil," "graveyard dust," as well as the bones of various animals and candles in a variety of shapes.

Mr. Ramos also has *black rag dolls (at $5 and $6), which are often sold along with a gold-plated sewing needle. The needles are stuck into the dolls to cause pain and discomfort to enemies* (italics mine).

Dolls of pleasure for some, dolls of pain for others—but indubitably all are dolls. It is difficult to refrain from writing that the more things change, the more they remain the same. When dolls have a dual function, so much the better for the owner who lies unprotected and prey to unknown terrors in the night: the evil eye of a childless neighbor, or the countless ills that science has not abolished—coughing, colds, mumps, measles, and a score of infections for impoverished mothers to combat. If you believe in "miracle" drugs, the panaceas promoted by the studio-dressed image of the friendly doctor, consider the tribeswoman who must do without a corner drugstore for the survival of her sick children. Her belief is, if you wish, childlike; her response is to the folklore of her people's ancient traditions. Of course, some will disparage both science and folkloric wisdom. Belief is not a pragmatic concept. Sickness and death are real, and so is the doll, whatever it may look like or however it is made.[20]

"It seems reasonable, during this age of constant exposure to sophisticated visual images, to believe that the spirit of man finally rebels and finds its excuse to manufacture simple art which is considered neither important nor lasting but fulfills a direct and urgent need in the individual. This need is sometimes satisfied by the annual ritual of creating colorful human effigies from whatever materials happen to be at hand."[21]

The author, Avon Neal, was writing of scarecrows, harvest figures, and snowmen—ephemeral folk figures that are still being made throughout rural America by farmers, housewives, and children. They are fashioned of sticks, cast-off clothing and rugs, hats, umbrellas, tin plates, fragments of glass, plastic masks, paper bags—the leftovers that one cannot in good conscience throw away. Practical country people employ these oddments to ward off not the evil eye but crows, groundhogs, and other despoilers of crops and gardens. Their invention is endless, the shapes fascinating and provocative. If these decaying symbols of man's authority over the birds and beasts last no more than a season, does their brief moment of life make them a less creative act than a monument in stone?[22] One prefers the scarecrow silhouette emerging phantom-like in the morning mist. And is this figure of magic, this effigy in scraps, not unlike the corn dollies still being made in rural England?[23] Its purpose is preservation, though its physical aspect is anything but serious.

For the child as well as the adult, the doll is a stimulus to realms of fantasy and reality; humanity's endless scenario of ideas and images takes as its point of departure, its "launching pad" into the unknown, the doll as goddess of love and beauty, a universal image that is the deepest expression of womankind of all ages and all races. The child's doll is man's extension of himself. It talks, crawls, walks, rolls its eyes, throws a ball into the air, drops its pants.[24] There are no rules to the game. It is a subtle, repetitive mimicry, a preparation for the world beyond the looking-glass.

That reality beyond the looking-glass is, for the grown-up world, a jungle of tangled prejudices. If it is too late, too complex, too difficult to untangle and create a clearing in the civilized jungle, how simple it is to return in memories, through the private ritual worship of the doll, to childhood and innocent beginnings. The pretense of belief and the abrogation of prejudice is childlike, acceptable without logical thought or tortuous reasoning. The transformation is swift—an enviable position for those who can maintain their pretense of belief without looking foolish or losing face. This may be the most difficult part of the game, and even it is often hedged with the "logical" persuasions of the collector, who justifies his passion by citing the doll's rarity,[25] cost, and price it will bring from a dealer. The economics of collecting are beyond the scope of this introduction,[26] but its attractions are certainly perennial. Every age re-creates its own ardent seekers after trifles or treasures in flea markets, thrift shops, and auctions. Hogarth might well have created a "Collector's Progress."

The joy and connoisseurship that surround the collector[27] are as palpable as the dolls he permits one to fondle. This is a blessing bestowed and humbly acknowledged; for while a doll in a locked case may be preserved for millions of visitors, an untouchable doll is only half an experience. Whatever the reasons for the repeated tableaux that I had begun to recognize as "The Adoration of the Collector," only this insatiable appetite for preserving and sharing makes any exhibition possible for the visitor less possessed with divine frenzy. A mixture of cupidity and love, the collectors' passion has preserved the so-called trivia of history. No

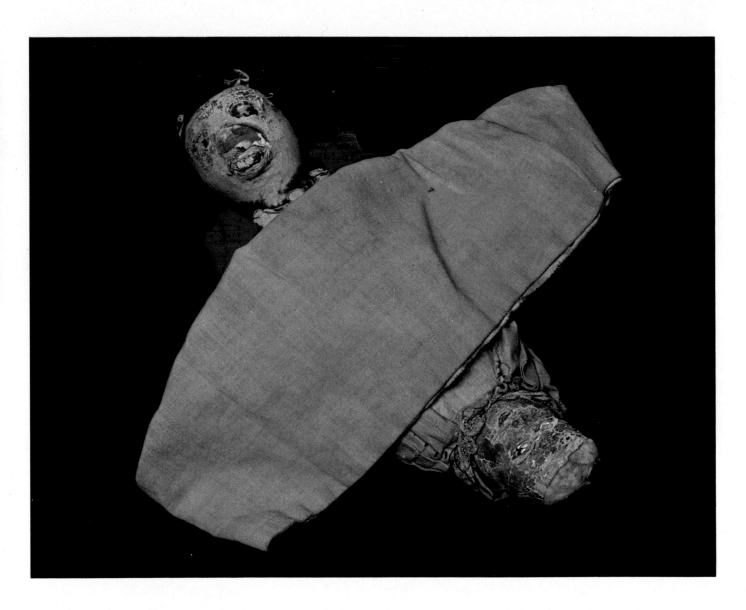

2. Those of us who scorn the idea that people in the twentieth century still believe in witchcraft and sorcery should consider our blind faith in newspaper pundits, television seers, and political soothsayers. This flagellation of reason may do more harm to a greater number than the hexing of a neighbor's horse or crop. The "witches," or as they are more commonly known in Pennsylvania today "powwowers," are adept at curing warts and will also "try for" (curing) wildfire (erysipelas), various wasting diseases, shingles, migraine, and any other human ailment. Our Pennsylvania German "hex" doll has heads of kid and body of rags. You have a choice of a pig's head or a human head. One cures warts and the other casts spells. These two have been well used, whether for good or evil we shall never know. Perhaps for both? Probably made about 1900, it measures 10¼ inches. *Collection Mary Merritt, Douglassville, Pa.*

memorable battles are here enshrined; no political questions or debates enter this playing field. Their appetite for history is limited to the commonplace, which, however we may deplore its vulgarity, makes up the experience of our world. "Every passion borders on the chaotic," wrote Walter Benjamin,[28] "but the collector's passion borders on the chaos of memories. . . . The most profound enchantment for the collector is the locking of individual items within a magic circle in which they are fixed as the final thrill, the thrill of acquisition, passes over them. Everything remembered and thought, everything conscious, becomes the

17

pedestal, the frame, the base, the lock of his property. . . . One has only to watch a collector handle the objects in his glass case. As he holds them in his hands, he seems to be seeing through them into their distant past as though inspired."

The collecting of dolls is not a new avocation, but it has become a full-blown passion for many thousands of people in this century. Perhaps this is true of collecting in general. As the population increases and the supplies diminish, the number of collectors increases geometrically. Certainly the paucity of information in the nineteenth century—the handful of books on dolls, the occasional dealer, and the rarity of dolls on display in museum collections—limited the audience for collecting the commonplace doll. The proliferation of special-subject books and an increase in the collecting of virtually everything have gone hand in hand within our lifetime. No matter which came first—the collector or the book—authentication of the doll was of primary concern to the collector groping for guidance. How old is the doll? Who made it? Where? His questions did not always receive satisfactory answers. Too many dolls have no oral or written history. Museums have often ignored the doll and the toy; how disappointed I have been to discover countless dolls on exhibition without labels or catalogue history.

Some people are born to be collectors. They are born to it even as magpies furnish their nests with "tremendous trifles." Often with modest funds for purchases, they must establish priorities and rules that are as restricting as the moves in a game of chess. The passionate collector is a person of courage, stubbornness, and pride of ownership. He delights in displaying his children to anyone with even the most casual interest. Time is forgotten as one is conducted on a grand tour of the collection. Places and pleasures of discovery are retold as an accompaniment to one's visual enjoyment.

As a child in Hungary, Louis F. Simon began collecting butterflies, which he preserved in boxes under his bed. At the age of six he was studying violin; at eleven he was a pupil at the Franz Liszt Conservatory in his native Budapest. In 1939 the Simons arrived in the United States. A professional musician at night, Simon spent his days in partnership with a zoologist stationed in Latin America who sent him monkeys, sloths, and jaguars which were sold to zoos and pet shops. (His garden today is home to one anteater and two rabbits for his young children.) In 1959, after his successful debut at Carnegie Hall, the State Department sent him as leader of his string quartet to India, Taiwan, Hong Kong, Korea, Ceylon, Cambodia, and Japan; the nucleus of his collection of Asiatic dolls was formed on this first of three trips.

The Simon house, which sits on a tree-lined knoll just over the New York City line, is from the outside like every other middle-class home in the suburbs. After climbing the steps one is uncertain of the similarity. A large, unpainted carrousel horse of about 1900 gallops noiselessly across the porch, where there are two school desks from about 1920. Beyond the glass doors the great hallway leads to a wide, winding staircase. The walls on either side of the hallway are lined with cases filled with artifacts and small sculptures; above them and along the staircase hangs a collection of masks from Africa, New Ireland, and New Guinea. I counted twenty-two. A scant dozen old kachinas stand colorfully along the top of a far case. We may describe this as the Simon introduction; the allegro follows, with the music room off the hallway on the right containing several cases of Oriental dolls. Musical instruments and Indonesian puppets decorate the walls. The living room opposite is host to a very large collection of Pre-Columbian, Asiatic, and Oceanic sculpture. There are Korean and Japanese chests,

3. A birthday gift to Mrs. Strong when she was five years old, this doll is a German bisque made about 1900, 16 inches high, with composition body, sleeping glass eyes, and hair gathered from Mrs. Strong's first haircut. She wears a dress of batiste and machine-made lace, with hand featherstitching where the lace joins the fabric. *Margaret Woodbury Strong Museum of Fascination, Pittsford, N.Y.*

Empire furniture, and one concession to contemporary lighting—a floor-to-ceiling paper lamp designed by the sculptor Noguchi. There are more cases and Oriental dolls in the dining room, and Oriental dolls in cases, drawers, and closets in the bedrooms. It was in the attic that I found the English puppet.

No rhyme, but reason enough for the visitor to marvel at each selection, which has been chosen with a keen eye for the authentic and the beautiful. There is no bowing to the whimsical fashions of the moment. What I saw in the collection was a portrait of a serious musician who has long enjoyed the old-fashioned virtues of discipline and training. A traditionalist who values the cultures of the past, he is equally occupied with creating an atmosphere for himself, his family, and his audience.

The alternate route of collecting is not available to most of us. Mrs. Homer Strong died just one month before we visited her collection in Rochester, New York. She left an estate estimated by the press at about one hundred million dollars. She also left a great deal more in the 35,000 to 50,000 dolls that overflow her rooms and cabinets. Coming upon them for the first time, even with warnings and much shaking of heads by not unbiased collectors, is like being buffeted by a raging snowstorm. One is in fact blinded by the multiplicity of examples staring at one from all sides. Nor is their attention ever diverted. The question hovers in the air: Who is regarding whom? Awe mingles with a profound feeling of inadequacy. No matter how often one peers into each case to separate the wheat from the chaff, one is never certain that all the dolls have been properly seen. How does one begin to select from what may be the largest private collection of dolls in the world? Nor were dolls all that Mrs. Strong collected. Seashells, minerals, toys, Orientalia, doll houses, bookplates . . . the number of things is staggering.

For the past twenty-two years, Mr. and Mrs. Irwin Hersey have lived in the same four-room apartment off Central Park. (Someday, someone must catalogue the unknown thousands of collectors who are hidden behind the anonymous facades of Greater New York. There is no way of knowing what is to be found beyond the identical apartment front doors.) Here one is instantly assaulted by a truly splendid profusion of sculptures, masks, and paintings. The pieces are small in scale, usually no larger than a handful, and everything may be lifted off the shelves, touched, and rubbed, as one instinctively does with sculpture in the hand.

The settings on numerous levels of shelves are variations on the installations by the noted designer and folk-art collector Alexander Girard. What could have been mad disarray falls into place, though there appears to be no logic to the juxtaposing of African, East Indian, Northwest Coast, South Pacific, Oriental, and Pre-Columbian from Mexico and Peru. It succeeds because each piece is a work of art collected for its unique beauty and not for its ethnographic history. Why one doll was selected and not another, one African carving and not a similar one, may never be satisfactorily explained or understood; familiarity with each piece as it relates to each collector's life-style may be the only clue. With Mr. Hersey it began when he was a Japanese-language officer working with United States Army Intelligence in Japan at the end of World War II. His first, tentative purchases were of Japanese prints found in bookshops at a time when more ambitious Occupation forces were "liberating" vast quantities of classical Japanese art. After the Korean War, when he again served in Japan, Mr. Hersey returned to the United States and began collecting unknown contemporary American painters and sculptors. His introduction to African art was in the studio of the photographer Arnold Newman. He neither understood nor liked what he saw. But in 1955, at a small auction house in New York, he bought an Eskimo ivory carving and a bronze from Dahomey, Africa. His knowledge of primitive art—"We don't have a word in our language to properly define 'primitive' art, and I prefer to use primitive and Pre-Columbian (which was anything but primitive) instead of indigenous or tribal arts"—has been a slow acculturation to varied histories and styles and the visual evaluation of the great pieces he can vividly recall in numerous private and public collections. Acquiring primitive art has been a serious pursuit. (The Herseys believe that their collection of Ibo and Ibibio masks and carvings from Nigeria may be the largest in the United States.)

Both the Herseys collect dolls, primarily Japanese and African. One of the two dolls in the traveling exhibition of African sculpture that was assembled by William Fagg of the British Museum in 1969 came from the Hersey collection. A memorable mistake they made was in not buying an eighteenth-century Japanese bunraku puppet because they thought it too expensive. If it were available today—and it is not—the same puppet would be ten times the original price. Mrs. Hersey, who never played with dolls as a child, bought her first one as an adult. It was an African Ashanti doll.[29] When it was purchased, there were few to be found; now this doll has become almost as commonplace in the world of primitive art as Raggedy Ann. Fifteen years after the initial purchase of African art, the Herseys surround themselves with a diverse and choice collection of individual pieces. One never seems to see it all. Each visit brings forth new pieces, new dolls that one would be willing to swear one had never seen before.

My own return to the past was due in great part to the flickering images of the movies. It was creative in the sense that my world of make-believe was stimulated to improvise on the events and people which were revealed to me on the screen's canvas. My belief was total. I recall the end of a picture when the house lights were brightened and I ran to look behind the screen for the people and places which had so magically vanished. Nor have I forgotten how awkwardly I stood and how I turned to my small companions, but could not speak to them of my ignorance. The city child went to the movies every Saturday morning. He saw everything. It was never necessary to ask about the baggy-suited, rakishly derby-hatted, cane-snapping Charlie Chaplin. His image on the movie poster was cause for noisy celebration. We understood and laughed, or did not understand and laughed anyway.[30]

Besides Chaplin, I remember one other figure of my Saturdays. Why I went or why it was shown in a neighborhood movie house, I have never understood. It was, I discovered many years later at the Museum of Modern Art, *The Golem*, a German movie made in 1920.[31] And my first foreign film, at age eight. Here was a doll larger than lifesize, created by a man, Rabbi Löwe, cabalist and alchemist. It was fashioned of clay, and the magic of life was concealed behind a six-pointed star on the Golem's broad chest. His stiff, slow movements were much like those of a mechanical doll. I remember his awesome face, his severe, angular cheekbones and bitter lips, and the hair that resembled a helmet. I remember, too, the Golem picking up a child who had given him an apple. The Golem smiles, and the child, playing with the star, accidentally removes it. The Golem falls lifeless to the ground![32] This was indeed the stuff of my dreams. As an only child, overwhelmed with toys, I spent my days transforming the toy images to imaginary, moving adventures. Soldiers, mechanical trains, animals, and paper dolls, all were cast into my Golems, imbued with life and death, which I generously distributed.

And so my images became real, and during the moments of invention, reality and make-believe were blurred; they dissolved and were transformed beyond reality. For me, these creative fantasies of childhood are recalled and stored in the glass cases of my private collections. Growing up and growing older changes very little. Today the world of toys and dolls is no less evocative. If anything, it is less cruel, more romantic. I see dolls in people and people in dolls. I fall in love with utter abandon and delight. I embrace all the strange, mad, beautiful, sad, lonely figures of shadow and substance, the collections that remind me of the innocent and heartfelt remark of Mrs. Gamp: "If I could afford to lay all my feller creeturs out for nothink, I would gladly do it, sich is the love I bears 'em."[33] And such is the collector's love, afford it or not, to capture in quantity the shining rows of porcelains and bisques, that one cannot accuse him of avarice or monopoly. His concern is evident. The multiplicity of dolls is a reflection only of an unfulfilled desire to protect his specimens from falling into less deserving hands![34]

This profusion of dolls suggests the everyday appearance of man in the mass. It is how we best know him—in his fruitfulness. It is upon reflection that the sparse collection almost becomes something precious and overly refined. There comes a time in every collector's life when he must cringe at the trumpeting cry of "good taste." It is something very special, this devotion to dolls. Unlike buttons and lace, paintings and prints, glass and china, stamps and coins, there is a profound loneliness to be found behind the innocence of a doll's eyes which is reflected in the love and loneliness one can often observe in the eyes of a collector.

In the collector's hall of fame is a select group of Europeans whose creations are venerated much as are old master paintings. Bru, Jumeau, Rohmer, Steiner, Huret, Montanari—they represent the élite, the haughty aristocrats of late nineteenth-century doll making. The French elegance of style was extended to the luxurious accessories of jewelry, furs, gloves, hats; their precise miniaturization of French fashion plates was a triumph of traditional craftsmen and women. Legends die hard, but the legendary beauty of Jumeau's numerous lady dolls and Bébés cannot be questioned. Their appeal is universal. As early as 1849 they were receiving medals. Wherever Jumeau dolls were exhibited—Paris, London, Vienna, Philadelphia, New Orleans, Melbourne—gold medals and diplomas were showered on these loveliest of bisque dolls. Other dolls may have more character, look more or less realistic, look like your baby, a child next door; for me, the physical beauty of Jumeau's dolls has not been surpassed. Not by his Parisian competitor Bru, whose superbly crafted dolls are attractive but do not attain the ineffable quality I associate with Jumeau. The rivalry among these esteemed doll makers of France—Leon Casimir Bru, Jules-Nicholas Steiner, Mlle. Calixte Huret, Mlle. Marie Antoinette Léontine Rohmer, and Pierre-François Jumeau—undoubtedly contributed to their preeminence and to the zeal with which they obtained patents for new mechanical improvements—a crying doll, an eating doll, a double-faced doll, a nursing doll, a doll's head that could move in all directions, movable eyes and eyelids, a musical doll, a breathing doll whose chest could simulate rhythmic inhaling and exhaling, as well as dolls that walked, talked, and threw a kiss.

Across the English Channel, Mme. Augusta Montanari ·was awarded a prize medal at the London Exhibition of 1851 for her "remarkable and beautiful collection of toys . . . a series of [wax] dolls representing all ages, from infancy to womanhood. . . . In a small case adjoining the wax dolls are displayed several rag dolls which are very remarkable productions."[35] Mary Hillier, in her book *Dolls and Doll-Makers*, suggests that the Montanaris may have come from Mexico, for it was at the same 1851 exhibition that Napoleon Montanari, Augusta's husband, displayed "full-sized models in wax of Mexican Indians."[36] The wax dolls of Montanari and Pierotti, another London-based doll maker, were not too dissimilar; those of both had wax heads, arms, and legs. Perhaps the foremost modeler in wax was Mme. Tussaud (1760–1850), who established her Wax Museum in Baker Street, London, in 1833. Her lifesize effigies, portraits of the famous and infamous, were technical prototypes of the wax dolls made by Montanari and Pierotti, which required the same skill and artistry. Is it only the size that makes the difference between a ghoulish figure and a charming doll? The preservation of the distinguished dead in a too-realistic medium has so far deterred me from visiting a waxworks, and I hope that no one will be inspired to reproduce the Tussaud gallery in miniature.

It is a long ocean voyage from the sophistication of the French doll to the humble American doll printed on cotton and sold singly or by the yard for cutting and stuffing. This idea, which hindsight makes appear inevitable, occurred to Celia and Charity Smith, of Ithaca, New York, in 1889. The drawing of their dolls is awkward and stiff, as is any pattern drawing, and the lithographic colors are much like those of calendar art; in short, they are commercial primitives of limited artistry. But they were a tremendous popular success and spawned innumerable imitations, for such cutouts were cheap and could fill a child's lonely days. The Smith ladies were—like all great inventors—in the right place at the right time. Their partnership produced several flat cutout dolls, among which was a Tabby Cat, printed by the Arnold Print Works in 1892, which has been successfully revived by a toy company in South Carolina.

Industry has a keen sense about the great buying public, and the larger the audience, the greater their desire to produce "what the public wants." Along with a mountain of forgotten trivia are a number of fondly remembered stuffed dolls offered by manufacturers: Aunt Jemima, Uncle Mose, and their two children, Diane and Wade; Kookie the Gas Range Man; Puffy, a Quaker Puffed Wheat soldier; the Cream of Wheat Chef; Sunny Jim; Ceresota Flour; and many others. My favorite cutouts remain the dozen saucy Brownies designed by the talented illustrator Palmer Cox, which were part of my childhood. Though they ought to seem grotesque, with their heads dissolving into narrow sloping shoulders, their silly, grinning faces, and popeyes, the Brownies remain for me very real people. I believe in their immortality, and in epochs hence they will astonish archaeologists digging into the substrata of the twentieth century.

It was a logical development from the do-it-yourself cutout to the manufactured rag doll whose face was stiffened with muslin. But professional competence alone does not create a masterpiece in this genre. How does one explain the spell cast on me by Miss Izannah Walker's rag dolls? The discriminating collector, author, and curator John Noble writes that "the first notable American-made dolls seem to be the rag dolls of Izannah Walker, of Central Falls, Rhode Island. . . . They are an entirely new concept in dollmaking, unlike anything made in Europe at that time."[37] An American primitive. Who was her model? Was it a self-portrait in which she did what most artists do—unconsciously modeled her own head? Round and absurdly simple, the painted features express a dignity of spirit in doll after doll; the purity of the oval shape reminds me of Giotto's apocryphal drawing of a perfect circle. Miss Walker was concerned with perfection only insofar as it produced a fair quantity of honest dolls. I am intrigued by her mechanical astuteness. In a letter to the *Providence Bulletin*, a niece of Miss Walker wrote: "Family tradition tells of her struggle to perfect her work and of the long wrestling with one problem, how to obtain a resistant surface to the stockinette heads, arms, and legs, without cracking or peeling. With this problem on her mind, Aunt Izannah suddenly sat up in bed one night to hear a voice say 'use paste.' It worked. . . . Aunt Izannah always deplored the fact that she was not a man. However, she made dolls and doll furniture, tinkered with household gadgets, designed a parlor heater 'that beat Ben Franklin's,' raised canaries, dabbled in real estate and was looked upon with admiration by male contemporaries because of her skill with carpenters' tools, so perhaps she was resigned. She used her own hand press and dies for the shaping of her dolls' heads and bodies; all of the little hands and feet were hand-sewn."[38]

Unlike Miss Walker, whose single note was sustained throughout, was Frau Käthe Kruse, who developed a varied production as she improved her patents for stuffed dolls' bodies. Her market was international, but the Käthe Kruse dolls made the deepest impression on the boys and girls of Germany. Her dolls achieve a sympathetic realism uncommon in the history of the doll. Lacking the cloying sweetness that most manufacturers provide their public, the Kruse dolls are recognizable as *children*. "The human hand cannot make exactly the same thing twice and everything on and about the dolls is handwork. How the little head is set on—this way or that—whether the hair or the eyes are painted light or dark . . . everything makes a different character and yet they have something in common. *Each doll goes through my hands at least twenty times!*"[39] So wrote Käthe Kruse in 1912, five years after she had made

4. Part of the genius of American manufacturers lies in their imaginative efforts to reach the buying public. The Northwestern Consolidated Milling Co. distributed their Ceresota cutout rag boy doll sometime after 1895. His broad shoulders, homely suspenders, farmer's boots, and round cap make him an advertising symbol to inspire confidence. Operation Bootstrap may have begun here! Today, the Ceresota boy would be representing his company in the local bowling league. He is 16 inches high. *Collection Margaret Whitton, Bridgewater, Conn.*

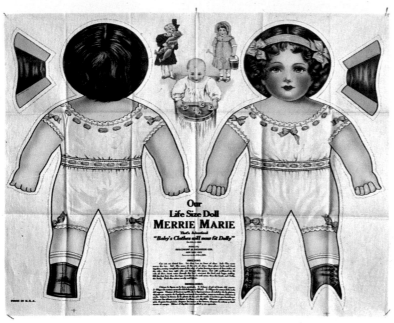

5. Edgar G. Newell patented his ''lifesize'' cutout rag dolls at the turn of the century. Merrie Marie, 24 inches high, has all the charm of a lithograph by Currier and Ives, and a take-me-or-leave-me expression which is common to most rag dolls of the period. Like them, she is a well-fed example of how middle-class Americans saw themselves. *Collection Margaret Whitton, Bridgewater, Conn.*

the crudest dolls out of toweling for her children.

Prejudices run deep. Am I alone in my eccentric tastes? If one searches long enough, other voices can be found reporting on the commercial malaise, a complaint not of our times alone. In *Harper's Bazaar* of the early 1880s an observer wrote: "It cannot be said that the modern progress of the doll toward artificial being has an elevating tendency on the young. . . . The doll of to-day is either a source of amusement or inordinate vanity. Even if endowed with an interior phonograph, and thus enabled to reproduce the human voice in any amount of speech, it must become a mere toy, stripped of its moral teaching."[40] American manufacturers were no different from their European and Japanese competitors. They were not interested in moral precepts, but were absorbed with introducing new models and new patents and with increasing production. If they could not match the beauty of the French and German dolls, their procession of doll models nonetheless seemed as inexhaustible as their customers. And though we have found little to illustrate by contemporary doll manufacturers, there is every reason to believe that among their thousands of designs someone will find what we have overlooked.

The manufacturing history of the doll is as fascinating as it is complex. And it is the mass-produced doll, whether made in the rural cottage or manufactured by the hundreds of thousands (or, more often, the tens of millions) in the urban factory, that is still available to the average collector.

One must begin with wooden dolls, because wood has been available in all countries of the doll-making world. Indeed, wooden dolls must be as old as wood-whittling man. Perhaps much older. Man undoubtedly found branch and twig formations shaped like himself and his children even before he taught himself the skills necessary to shape the human form. While the cave paintings of Altamira and Lascaux were preserved by natural climatic conditions, both nature and man have destroyed any vestiges of wooden prehistoric dolls.

Wooden dolls were made in quantity in England and France, and distributed in the Middle European countries by enterprising peddlers well before the eighteenth century. The peddlers carried their wares of toys and dolls (called Babies) and puppets on their broad backs, by packhorse, and by sailing ships. But by far the greatest existing number of wooden dolls are those made in Germany and Austria in the seventeenth and eighteenth centuries. Sonneberg in Thuringia, Berchtesgaden in Bavaria, and Grödner Tal in the Austrian Tyrol soon became the largest centers of production and distribution. An early catalogue from Nuremberg (1793–1807) depicts wooden dolls that were probably made in Grödner Tal and Sonneberg. Of the 132 dolls Queen Victoria dressed and played with as a child, most were inexpensive jointed woodens. Of those listed in her copy book, thirty-two were dressed by the young princess, and the remainder by her governess, Baroness Lehzen. They can be seen today in Kensington Palace. For those who are content to do their traveling via rocking chair or library, there is *Queen Victoria's Dolls* by Frances Low (London: G. Newnes, 1894).

Long before their recorded history began, dolls were shaped from cloth, bone, stone, and clay. The museums of the world have in their collections a fascinating range of Neolithic images of female figures whose use can only be conjectured. They are catalogued as idols. We flatter ourselves in believing that progress is equated with modern man, and that these crude, often abstract shapes were made by a childlike people whose entire waking and sleeping lives were spent in fear of the unknown. If they were childlike, then these primitive people must have spent some less fearful moments playing with their simply formed toys and dolls. Then as now, the preponderant doll shape was female, and the male doll a rarity. If man was, then as now, the prime artificer, the dominant but underground role that the female has assumed in history has not changed. Her image, whether as goddess or doll, plays the primary role in the life of her children.

Not until the commercial floodgates were opened for the mass-production and distribution of the doll did it become accepted as a child's toy and plaything. But that did not begin until the eighteenth century, when the efficiently organized German craftsmen merchandised their production throughout Europe and America at prices almost everyone could afford. Those who could not, or who lived in areas too remote even for itinerant peddlers, made their own dolls of wood and rags. The economically fortunate could indulge their fancies by ordering from abroad, as did George Washington, who wrote to England for "a neat dress'd Wax Baby!" for his stepdaughter. Washington's expenditure was modest compared to the munificent sums lavished on dolls by European royalty and those who could afford to seek favors of royalty. The young Dauphin was the recipient of a "state coach filled with dolls." Cardinal Richelieu presented to the Duchesse d'Enghien six dolls which comprised a family in miniature: grandmother, mother, child, midwife, nurse, and lady's maid. What delicacy of feeling prevented the inclusion of a husband? Louis XV, or the Duchesse d'Orléans in the king's name, presented to the princess who was soon to become queen of France a doll with a voluminous wardrobe which in those preinflationary days cost them over 20,000 francs. No doubt this was following in the best French tradition. As early as 1321, the queen of France sent a doll dressed in the latest French fashions to the queen of England, wife of Edward II. The sensation it created at the English court has been a boon to French dressmakers these past 650 years!

Max von Boehn's dour comments on French "duplicity" deserve mention. "More skilfully than any other nation the French utilized dolls as a profitable means of propaganda, employing them freely in the service of their trade in ladies' fashions. French fashions, and not by chance, are highly favoured by women of all the five continents. Yet only rarely are these fashions real inventions of Paris; usually they come from other sources; but there they are executed with so much taste, and the French women know how to wear their clothes with such a peculiar charm, that Paris fashions capture all eyes and are eagerly imitated. The French never spare themselves self-praise, and just as something always remains in the mind when we hear slander of others, so this general and constantly repeated self-praise never misses its mark. . . . To the doll was given the task of popularizing French fashions abroad."[41]

It was Jean-Baptiste Colbert, minister of finance to Louis XIV (1643–1715), who along with his king established the French textile industries. Colbert summed it up quite succinctly: "French fashions are to France what the mines of Peru are to Spain." Obviously the French were not born to this supremacy. It required patronage, direction, ambition, and the resplendent atmosphere of court life which encouraged high fashion through a succession of masques and balls. Certainly nothing else in man's history so points up the theory of built-in obsolescence. Fashions are mercurial, whimsical, and ravishing to man and woman alike. Feminine costume in France was of a brilliance unmatched in the courts of Europe. Pompadour, Du Barry, and Marie Antoinette were fashion's leaders, whose variants of dress and headdress provoked the feverish activity of dressmakers and milliners. The wives of the court nobles waited for a sign and then were off in mad pursuit. What remains more or less constant is the human body, its change dictated by male society's preference for fat or thin, for revealing or hiding the contours beneath the dress. Upon this framework was built fashion's enthusiasm for conspicuous consumption.

The looking-glass images of French fashion history are reflected in each kingly succession and revolutionary upheaval. Even before 1789, the prosperous middle class was waiting in the wings for its entrance into society. But it was not until the late 1830s that trade, manufacture, and money began their assault upon, and ultimate conquest of, French cultural and industrial life. The Second Empire of Napoleon III saw the introduction of couture, competitive fashion houses, and the modeling of clothes by living models from which the fashionable selected their garments. The continuing dependence on dolls for the promotion of the latest fashions increased with the rise of the middle class throughout Europe and the colonies. As the Colemans suggest, the so-called fashion doll was not "a type of doll but rather a functional use of dolls. Nearly any type of doll could be dressed in the latest adult or children's fashions and be sent out to show current styles."[42] In about 1850, Natalis Rondot was writing that "the cloak and the dress of a little doll costing but 20 cents are perfectly correct reproductions of our newest fashions. . . . The doll is hurried off to the provinces and often to foreign lands as patron of the fashions; she has even become an indispensable accessory for all the latest novelties and it is now the case that without a doll, merchants would find it difficult to sell their wares. The first cloaks that were sent to India were worn by the ladies of Calcutta on their heads, like mantillas, until the doll-models arrived to show the fashion."[43]

The Colemans, to whom all doll collectors must be forever grateful, forthrightly speak their mind: "French dolls are among the most artistic ever created."[44] How much of this was owing to their unrivaled beauty of dress? And just as Paris fashions are soon found in our department stores at reduced prices and with inferior styling, so did the French fashion doll make its way to the aspiring seventeenth-century bourgeoisie of Europe. Nor were the latest styles in hairdressing overlooked; dolls were coiffed to instruct the hairdresser as well as the owner of the doll.

The first metal doll parts were manufactured in France and Germany. Heads, legs, and hands were made of copper, zinc, brass, lead, tin, pewter, and aluminum. This flurry of activity began in the 1860s. Not until the late 1870s did the Americans patent their metal dolls. Although rubber had been employed by doll makers in various countries for centuries prior to the birth of the Goodyear Rubber Company, it was not until the vulcanization process was patented by Charles Goodyear in 1844 that the doll of rubber could be depended on to hold its shape. Commercial production soon followed. But perhaps the single most popular material for the doll has been glazed porcelain or high-fired china. The inexpensive china heads and legs were first made to be mounted on the equally inexpensive peg woodens. It was later in the century, about 1876, that the small, all-bisque jointed dolls made in Germany and commonly known as Frozen Charlottes found their way to the toy counters and peddlers of Europe.

The birth of the granddaddy of our plastic doll civilization is credited to the production of celluloid in Newark, New Jersey, in 1869, by the Celluloid Novelty Company. My generation is old enough to remember the popularity and cheapness of celluloid dolls. Indeed, I must never have known a celluloid doll of quality. I recall how easy it was to press their too-fragile bodies between my fingers and listen to them crack. But one was not prompted to destroy the doll that was offered by Bru in France about 1870. These ball-jointed composition bodies were strung with elastic, while the joints were made of wood; they were called the *Bébé Incassable*.

Realism in the manufacture of the nineteenth-century doll achieved its greatest success

6. It is no coincidence that these Brownie dolls are to be found in the collection of Mrs. Homer Strong, whose father was an early investor in Kodak. The Brownies, copyrighted in 1892 by Palmer Cox, remain an American classic. Do you remember (in alphabetical order) John Bull, Canadian, Chinaman, Dude, German, Highlander, Indian, Irishman, Policeman, Sailor, Soldier, and Uncle Sam? They are 7½ inches high. Front and back were printed to be cut out, stuffed, and sewn together. Some say that the Brownie camera was named after them. Others say that the name could have originated with Frank Brownell, who manufactured the camera—first offered for sale in 1900—or that it came from George Eastman's pet dog Brownie. *Margaret Woodbury Strong Museum of Fascination, Pittsford, N.Y.*

with the Edison phonograph doll. Throughout the ages, inventive man has endeavored to give voice and movement to his inanimate creations. "The ancient Egyptians," wrote Naville in 1906, "not only believed that gods spoke to each other; they also accepted the incantations supposedly pronounced by Thoth as if it were the god himself who had spoken to them. Furthermore, they made statues speak, and had prophetic images who intervened on many occasions in their lives."[45] Another Egyptologist has written that at Thebes there were statues that spoke and made gestures. "The priests made the heads and arms move by devices not as yet clearly explained."[46] This illusion of reality was not a deceit practiced by magicians for its value as secular entertainment. The "representation of the act *is* the act itself."[47]

A true walking figure was designed by the Jesuit priest Gabriel de Magalhaens when he was a missionary in China. "One day he offered the great Emperor, Kang'hi, a statue operated by interior springs, which walked for a quarter of an hour, with a drawn sword in its right hand and a shield on its left arm."[48] His religious intentions are questionable, and whatever effect his feat may have had on the emperor, it did not deter him, in 1662, from torturing De Magalhaens and his fellow priests.

Manufacturers have long sacrificed their craft skills to mass-production and sales. The Colemans write that "the production figures for dolls stagger the imagination."[49] Their estimates, which begin for the year 1844 and conclude with 1925 and cover Germany, France, and the United States, are but a sampling of some major doll companies. What can one say about "20,000,000 papier-mâché dolls' heads made in Sonneberg"[50] in 1903? Or one German factory operating from 1754 to 1884 producing a billion china dolls? A surreal picture of nondisposable plastic dolls joining the wastelands of nondisposable automobiles and nonreturnable cans and bottles is not without plausibility. The ecological implications, however, are not as forbidding. Nor is the return to handcraftsmanship a viable economic consideration in an overpopulated world of eager purchasers. What the developing doll manufacturers of the nineteenth century contributed was a specialization of detail which could be perfected for maximum sales to an ever-expanding public. The range of mechanical changes and new materials was the direct result of private enterprise seeking new world markets.

The search for quality has no effect on the sales or popularity of today's television specials. Cries of outrage go unheeded as long as the criticism is confined to aesthetics and speculative arguments. The marketplace ignores the conceits and quibbles of taste, offering no choice between a "classic" doll and a potboiler. Plastics and synthetics replace wood, lead, paper, tin, iron, papier-mâché. Other times, other media. What many have named the inevitable march of progress, others in violent disagreement have damned as meretricious. But can we not hear faint echoes repeating in each generation the same cries of despair and indignation? The banner words Tradition! Beauty! Childhood! Craftsmanship! So many Villons asking, "Where are the snows of yesteryear?" So many grown older, who equate beauty and craftsmanship with the past.[51] The arguments for supporting one or the other side are easy to assemble. My sympathies, as I search vainly to recapture the early mornings of childhood, are with the romantic Villons. Quality is a *rara avis*, elusive in every age. Because the world thrives on limited talents, popularity should not be joined with longevity, or what the trade calls its "staples."

Standards of taste demand sensitive guides. I would argue that such guides must educate within the cycles of profit and loss, the cause and effect of all commercial ventures regardless of size. If they tested their taste and value judgments against the culturally circumscribed but pragmatic experience of the business world, they could create a partnership of the best in theory and practice. Who knows how much is lost every year in time, money, and effort by the production of shoddy, vulgar, badly designed dolls. Or how much is lost by vague and hopeful speculations. The business world may adopt a pragmatic approach, but that is wasteful and self-defeating because of its limitations. When the only direction and goal is a marked-down version of an imitation, or an overripe adult image of what the manufacturer thinks every mother and child think is the perfect doll for a child, then the chances for failure must be statistically greater than the number of successful promotions. Given the concept of creating a doll and the means for developing it, it is open to question whether any two people will totally agree. And yet, the amalgam of both points of view suggests the imaginative potential of the new doll, whatever she may become. In any cooperative selection there will always be a gathering of the safe and sound. There can also be aspects of the unknown, the inexplicable, which can provoke controversy as well as affection. For man and doll to be remembered, there must be some strangeness, even a gleam of madness or eccentricity, and genius of character.

A walk through the toy and department stores in search of dolls has the cumulative effect of producing severe depression. The shifting fads of fashion—that illusory "carrot" dangled by the advertising industry—are mirrored by the doll manufacturers with some success and indifferent merchandise. Perhaps it was always so; perhaps the merchandise of the eighteenth, nineteenth, and early twentieth centuries had no more to offer, and the quality we find in collections today represents but a meager percentage of the mediocre whole. If this is so, then our contemporary scene must be looked upon as one of the less flourishing periods from which, hopefully, a modest number of dolls will survive into the next century. For those of us who are intrigued by the proliferation of Pop art styles based on soup cans and cartoon strips, it is with a feeling of déjà vu that we rediscover the Campbell Kids, who were first drawn in 1900 and later redrawn by Grace Drayton, whose dolls and drawings are similar in style to those of Rose O'Neill, with her immortal Kewpies. The roster of commercial dolls based on American cartoon characters is as varied as the tributaries of the Mississippi: Abe Kabibble, Annie Rooney, Brownies, Reg'lar Fellers, Happy Hooligan, Maggie and Jiggs, Buster Brown, Buttercup, Dolly Drake, Fluffy Ruffles, Foxy Grandpa, Little Mary Mix-Up, Skeezix, Little Nemo, Little Orphan Annie, Little Snookums, Lord Plushbottom, Puddin Head, and a few commercial products such as Spearmint Kids (with "Wrigley" eyes), Uneeda Kid, and Zu-Zu Kid, an aspect of American grass roots culture which has been overlooked, and which deserves a doctoral thesis and installation in a museum of American history. And if they are still to be found in someone's collection, one should like to see included in the same exhibition Suffering Suffragette, Suffragette Kid, and Suffragina.[52]

The cartoon strip in the daily newspapers, as much as it has changed from the innocence of the early cartoons, continues to be read more widely than the news. There is an estimated worldwide audience of six to seven hundred million readers weekly. No wonder the manufacturers' enthusiasm for repeating such a tried popular success! "In 1960, a Boston University study chronicled the march of business into the world of the comics..... 'Enterprising manufacturers have found a gold mine in the comic strips. Merchandise, particularly in the form of dolls and toys, inspired by comic strip characters have had nothing but success.' "[53]

And what of the future, when dolls as we have known them will be joined with the newest technology and ultimately result in the nondoll, the nonhuman, the nonrepresentational, amorphous, nontoxic cloud? It has its advantages. In a world hard pressed for space there will no longer be a need for storage. Nothing will have to be saved. Collecting will have either vanished from the earth or become a frenzied scene of hands clutching even at straws. Today, the creator-manufacturers are advancing new trends, new laboratory experiments on non-collectible objects in space.[54] The real merges with the unreal into an undefined, inconclusive state of perception. One walks carefully and listens to the critical and esoteric voices.

The new synthetics, which are still in their infancy, will, in more creative hands, be used to develop the doll or dolls that will outlast the fashions of their immediate time and place. The past few years bring to mind no nominations for immortality. The field of choice is small. What is found in one store or mail-order catalogue can be found in all the others. There are few happy surprises. Greater offenders are the unimaginative and often ugly puppets that embody the worst aspects of design and manufacture. More love, understanding, and sculptural quality are given to the mohair and plush animals—which may be why so many children prefer to play with animals rather than dolls. Is the animal basically more interesting than the human? Certainly animals have greater variety in color, shape, and markings. Nevertheless, our human condition demands the fantasy of love, which only a doll can gratify.

The neuterization of dolls[55] is a curious tradition to continue in this age of laissez-faire attitudes toward sex. Magazines and movies blatantly expose acres of technicolor flesh. Because of their haste to arouse and excite, their end product has nothing to do with literature or motion-picture art. Sex has become commercial entertainment, available to anyone who can flip the pages or afford the admission. What is revealed is produced because it has long been forbidden, and because ignorance is not bliss—it is an irritant.

The doll's evasion of man's anatomy is in question because it is unnatural. As with the nose on one's face, repetition of their existence must create the inevitable acceptance of the reality of sexual organs, putting them into their true human perspective—of neither more nor less interest than other parts of our anatomical landscape. Unlike "exotic natives," we spend all our lives in clothes, day or night clothes. In-between nakedness is brief, and nudity soon palls. Nor can it ever be as elegant as a properly dressed doll, or as dear to one as a familiar, ragged dress. The doll has been a euphemistic symbol of little boys and girls. In truth, they have been interchangeable except for their hair, which in today's dolls often has the same fullness of wig.

That there are distinctive and different sexual characteristics for boys and girls had been an adult secret not readily shared with children. But secrets will out—and we owe its release to those sexually emancipated French who distributed in the United States the "anatomically correct" boy doll Petit Frère, or Little Brother.[56] Designed by Mme. Refabert and manufactured by her husband, Claude, Little Brother had as its source of inspiration Verrocchio's statue of a cherub with a dolphin in the Palazzo Vecchio in Florence.[57] "In physical detail, the Little Brother doll is all boy. This abrupt departure from neuter kewpie-doll bodies, which we've all grown used to from time immemorial, may shock some adult shoppers taken unawares."[58]

Unfortunately, the reduction from a Renaissance sculpture to a contemporary doll added nothing to the history of dolls other than its anatomical depiction. It is neither beautiful nor unforgettable, and while vinyl may make the new dolls unbreakable, this synthetic is regrettably unpleasant to the touch. But this pebble of doubt cast into the pool of memory must create disturbing ripples in each adult's probing of his childhood. How often has it been questioned by a child, as it was by Refabert's grandson when, picking up a doll, he asked his grandmother, "Is it a boy or a girl?" The chances are excellent that it should be one or the other—but which one? Kewpies had no answer. Neither had any of the countless dolls that had been stood on their heads and examined by generations of curious boys and girls. It is the primal human question which we do our best to ignore, pretending there is no answer. Instead, we celebrate the functions of our sexless dolls with their ability to wet and to cry "real" tears. The inquiring child of a scientific century may soon demand *real* uric acid! One may also ask: "What next?" It depends on the synthesis of the social scene and the accounting department. Manufacturers cannot be averse to joining each bandwagon as it appears. Commercial reality offers them no alternative. This commonplace is as true for the manufacture of dolls as it is for the manufacture of automobiles. Similarity breeds not contempt but acceptance and economic security.

"To look at everything as if you saw it for the first time takes courage," said the painter Henri Matisse. To manufacture a popular commercial doll without precedent in the history of doll making is equally courageous. Little Brother was joined by Little Sister. Sexual equality had at last broken all human barriers.

Not only sexual equality has liberated the female sex. The day after Christmas was spent at the home of a friend, whose four-year-old daughter was playing with as well as demonstrating to Mother, Father, and me her mechanical plastic doll that walked across the carpet without human assistance. It clattered as it moved its stiff legs and we lost interest after acknowledging our wonderment at this accomplished blond walker. Much later, I noticed the doll on its stomach and the child unhinging a door in the center of the doll's back. Without crying for help, and frowning intently, the child removed two large batteries, shuffled them about mysteriously, replaced them, closed the door, and stood the doll on its feet; with utter indifference to its late mechanical failure, it walked across the room, followed by its skipping owner who shouted, "Fixed it! Fixed it! Fixed it!" I was enthralled. Nobody else paid the slightest attention to their mechanical prodigy. Not only has woman been emancipated (*sic*), but girls born of women now inherit and claim equal technical rights in what was once man's undisputed domain—as sometime slave and occasional master to the machine. So be it, and welcome to your new freedom—your right to lubricate and to remove and replace defective mechanical parts.

Styles and prejudices change but the human condition remains the same; sharing our prejudices we expose ourselves. Only the design within the structure varies in each generation. It was in 1947 that Negro author Ralph Ellison wrote: "I am an invisible man. . . . I am invisible, understand, simply because people refuse to see me. Like the bodiless heads you see sometimes in circus sideshows, it is as though I have been surrounded by mirrors of hard, distorting glass. When they approach me they see only my surroundings, themselves, or figments of their imagination—indeed, everything and anything except me."[59] The occasional black doll of the past was a sort of curio, the odd doll out, a sentimental depiction of the slave, servant, and minstrel man. The few exceptions are eloquent examples of people's ignoring the color prejudices of their time.

If it is understood that we have taken to our hearts all the dolls illustrated, it must also be understood that like any fond-foolish parent, we confess to having favorites. As he was tenderly removed by the curator at Newark[60] from his tissue-lined box, the Negro boy doll looked up at me. He was made of black alpaca and had black hair of fine, wispy mat. With jet-black eyes and velveteen trousers and shirt, he was all quite dark except for the white of his eyes, rimmed upward like the blade of a scimitar, and a shy smile revealing the tiniest white teeth. Marching down the front of his shirt, a pearly white procession of buttons winked at us. I could have watched him pass me every Sunday morning on his way to church a block from where I lived as a child. He walks between his mother and father, holding their hands. As our eyes meet I mean to smile, but never do. Many Sundays later, the thought occurs to me that he has moved away. There is no one on the quiet morning street to take his place.

Another favorite reflects Whitman's eulogy: "The commonplace I sing. . . ." Like most of us she is anonymous. She may be squashed and hugged, kicked and thrown about without suffering too great damage. She is a black doll knitted in red, white, and blue, and stands straight and dignified. Her shape is still firm, her legs faintly stout. She is dressed for a holiday and her round hat retains its jaunty snap-brim.[61] It was, for me, love at first sight. Of the numerous dolls I covet, she would be an important addition to my modest collection, which contains not a single black doll from the United States. An early acquisition was a mechanical dancing black man made of tin, whose long articulated legs beat out a jigging rhythm on a tin box. Instead of black dolls, I have at home a wide range of browns. There are small brown doll musicians from Surinam; brown occupational dolls from the Malagasy Republic, India, and Morocco; brown costume dolls from Guatemala and Mexico. Even the American Indian dolls are brown, as are the Otavalo Indian dolls from Ecuador. Curiously, a Navajo doll has a light pink face. What I have refused to collect are the white dolls with "white" features that have been painted black. The mold is the same, only the color has been added. They are Hollywood cute. But this banal concept is slowly beginning to change.

Authorities in the West have taken a rather long time to recognize that the "primitive" has also contributed to the plastic arts, and that much of his sculpture ranks with the great bronzes and wood carvings of our civilization. For civilizations long dead, the game of identifying them and their function continues to change with each generation. Within our memory, folk arts and the arts of Black Africa—to select only two examples—have been recognized and judged on their own merits and in terms related to their own societies. There is much in the known and unknown world that we distort because we lack sufficient knowledge born of direct experience. The symbolic language of African art requires of the novice a desire to learn a new language. It is a language with ever-increasing surprises of form and content. After some thirty-five years of looking at African art, I begin to understand that my knowledge is small; but my enthusiasm for the varied styles is greater than ever. It is too simplistic to characterize all African art as abstract, when one is confronted with the great realistic bronzes from Ife or the relatively more realistic bronze figures from Tada (both in Nigeria), which must be included in the humanist tradition. In the tenth century, at the same time that Middle Europe was fashioning doll-like figures of the Christian pantheon for its illiterate congregations, and Heian period Japan (794–1185) had the common custom of making paper and grass dolls on selected days of the year to exorcise life's physical misfortunes by rubbing these dolls over one's body, and Buddhist priests were using dolls to illustrate their texts for a population that could neither read nor write—in this same period, about the year 1000, the craftsmen of Nigeria were making bronze castings equal to those made later in Europe and the Orient. Man's uniqueness is not confined to the history of the East and West. The equivalent of what has been preserved of these cultures for our edification and delight was not preserved in sub-Sahara Africa, because of climate, religious practices, and colonial expansion.

The dolls we illustrate were not made by "artists." They represent but one small facet of complex social units in which every individual is an integral part of a social family. Moreover, none of us really can be certain whether some carvings were used as dolls. They are called figurines, idols, fetishes, ancestor figures because not enough was known by the early missionaries and explorers, who considered the objects merely as "curios" to be housed in ethnographic collections and studied as products of uncivilized man. What was once brought into the temple of art through the back door is now an accepted cultural fact. The placing of African dolls within the framework of doll history is the inevitable next step, made more difficult by the nature of the material (wood), whose life span under extreme climatic conditions may make it too late even now. The abundance of exhibitions and private collections must be augmented by a more popular approach, beginning, of course, with the inclusion of African art in the educational curriculum. A modest start can be made with the collecting of the dolls of Black Africa.

It was less than a century ago, in 1893, that the wood carvings called kachinas were exhibited at the World's Columbian Exposition in Chicago. There may not be anything else like them in the world of dolls. The diversity of form, color, character, and sheer visual excitement in the Hopi Indian kachinas creates an aura of mystery and beauty that is rarely met with in dolls or sculpture. Much of their fascination lies in their abstract, shorthand pictorialism, which leaves everything to the imagination. Realism as we know it is never attempted; color and shape are symbolic. All our notions about portraiture break down in observing the symbolic portraits of the Hopis and Zuñis. There is neither sentiment nor intimacy, flattery nor psychological penetration in the individual kachina, which is, after all, a *spirit* of a plant, animal, ogre, bird, or clown. Their identification is the Hopi child's homework. Instead of memorizing presidential portraits, he is expected to learn the names of the kachina dolls that are made by his father and uncles as guides to the naming of the adult kachina dancers[62] whose masks are the dolls' prototypes. "Children are given small figures carved of soft cottonwood roots, correctly painted and costumed to represent the masked impersonators. These 'dolls' are also called *kachinas* but are not invested with power; they serve only to help familiarize children with the masks and names of the real *kachinas*, as every Hopi child upon reaching the age of six to eight years must be initiated into either the Kachina or Powamu Society."[63]

Though I am ignorant of the Indians' religious motivations, I submit to the spiritual force of the kachina dolls: they seem to awaken a dormant, atavistic impulse to participate in their religious experience. I know intellectually that this cannot be so; there is nothing in my background to encourage identification with a people I have not met and a life-style of

7. A few years ago, Mary Anne McLean Bradford made a string of flat wooden dolls with joined hands which were cut away one by one until there remained only this "miniature scarecrow"; this icon, this happy essence of a plaything—which delights me as much as its owner, who dandles it on his knee for his visitors' approval—is 8 inches high. *Collection Mr. and Mrs. H. Landshoff.*

which I know nothing. Nor do I expect to join them in their night dances, for those are attended only by the kachina dancers, who enter the private world of the kiva, their underground ceremonial chamber. And though we know there is a human face behind each kachina dancer's mask, we brood on the mystery of what may lie behind the kachina doll's painted mask.

"The origin of Hopi kachinas lies far back in the prehistoric past. The Kókopilau Kachina sings a song in a language so ancient that not a word of it is understood by the modern Hopis, who know only that kachinas accompanied them throughout their migrations. Indeed, they assert that kachinas came up with them during their Emergence from the womb of Mother Earth."[64] This stubborn expression of a people's faith is found in many so-called primitive religions, but no people express themselves as vividly as the Hopis do through their kachina dolls. These stand like architectural columns, but within their sculpted rigidity the first earth-treading steps of their dance are anticipated. The paradox of movement where no movement exists is suggested by the outward thrust of arms and a fist clutching a gourd rattle. The dolls are without precedent and have become transformed into what I would call works of art.[65] Aside from them and some of the carvings from Africa, there are not many such works I would raise to this level. If I had ever thought of collecting, serious collecting, which paralyzes the will and destroys objectivity, my passion would have been directed toward the kachinas in all their multiplicity of invention. It is too late for the comparatively old dolls,[66] which are best seen in the museums and private collections of the Southwest, and for the kachinas that are displayed at the Museum of the American Indian; it is not too late for fine examples of newly carved and painted kachinas, which, though made for the tourist trade, should not be overlooked or scorned.[67] To select the new, one must immerse one's sensibilities in the old. Hopi tradition is a path on which the old and the new still walk together, if not side by side, at least in Indian file.

To the child, the doll is a *presence*. It is forever on the threshold of becoming, of being—of being whatever the child or adult breathes into it.[68] His utterances may be gibberish or cabalistic, and beyond the boundaries frozen by traditional concepts of meaning. The doll is a private vessel into which are distilled fears, hopes, sorrows, and magic make-believe. The diabolical is not less than the angelic. One begins with innocence, and the experience of time breeds knowledge and the power for good and evil. Time transforms the levels of play, which may be as secret as the confessional or as brash as theatricals to an audience coaxed with ice cream and cookies. Nothing and everything is revealed, the heart laid bare. "To this crib I always took my doll; human beings must love something, and in the dearth of worthier objects of affection, I contrived to find a pleasure in loving and cherishing a faded graven image, shabby as a miniature scarecrow. It puzzles me now to remember with what absurd sincerity I doated on this little toy, half fancying it alive and capable of sensation. I could not sleep unless it was folded in my night-gown; and when it lay there safe and warm, I was comparatively happy, believing it to be happy likewise."[69]

The elaborate doll pleases most the adult, who is charmed by the luxury of the costume. My wife recalls the dolls made by her mother, who, with the humblest materials, a rag or a scrap of toweling, would dexterously fold and knot for her a "dolly." She speaks of them with affection in no way diminished by time; one can actually see her psychic removal in time as she returns for a moment to her childhood dolls and, since she spent a great deal of time alone, her closest friends. One is constantly reminded of the child's utter simplicity of needs, a simplicity we ignore by supplying our children with an abundance of things because, I presume, we are fundamentally insensitive to their deeper needs. I suspect it is also a display of strength (or weakness) by which, through this form of unconscious and well-meaning blackmail, we ensure the child's dependency. Yet we are betraying the child by our casual withdrawals, which we justify for any number of reasons—work, cleaning, fatigue, television, bowling; and the child, left to herself, grasps at the only thing resembling a surrogate parent, her doll and constant companion.

My loneliness was mitigated by the concern of loving relatives. My weekly visit to Grandmother meant a ride on the trolley car, primly closed in winter but joyously open on all sides in summer. If one were lucky there might be an empty seat behind the motorman. And since I was alone and very young, he sometimes permitted me to stamp my foot on the warning bell beneath his foot when there was someone on the tracks. At Grandmother's there were little things to play with: a painted Noah's Ark with numerous wooden animals; a wooden horse and rider with a tail that was a whistle; a jumping jack who never tired of kicking his legs and arms; sepia pictures of overdressed children; candies; and nuts. When I brushed all this aside and yearned to return home, Grandmother would leave her chair opposite me, her severe black dress swishing across the wide-beamed kitchen floor. I would watch her reach to a high shelf and bring me the special companion of late Sunday afternoons, the painted wooden Nutcracker, with fierce mustache and a jointed mouth that would open and close for the remainder of my visit. For many years Sundays were Nutcracker days. Other memories have vanished, but Grandmother's Nutcracker, which I believed she shared only with me, has never been forgotten. When I began to search for toys and dolls for children, Nutcracker was on my "most wanted" list. Alas, when I found him, he no longer seemed the same, his mustache not quite so fierce, his jaw a trifle weaker. Never mind. He will always be associated with Grandmother—twin joys of cozy afternoons in a very old frame house under a noisy elevated railroad.

Who can tell at what moment the figure on a shelf becomes a child's plaything, toy, or doll? The beautiful porcelain lady, long coveted by the child who has been warned not to touch her, is freed by that child from adult bondage, and, pressed against her breast, is no longer an aloof statue but a playmate for secret games and intimate conversations. To be caught is to be punished: one must be stealthy and alert to danger. Surely, this moment is the end of innocence, the introduction to adult games whose rules for survival must be swiftly learned.

The metamorphosis of sacred objects into dolls is a pantomime that I suspect has been played out by children since the world began. On a recent visit to the American Museum of Natural History, I noted a label in a case of Pre-Columbian art: "Small ceramic figurines usually fragmentary and found in tremendous numbers in all parts of Teotihuacan, were supposedly household idols of no great value . . . were made in molds . . . a mass production technique first introduced at this time." My eye and mind responded in unison. The figurines, were just the right size; they looked like dolls, and since they were in plentiful supply, no one scolded if the idols(?) were caressed, dressed, fed, and placed close to the child on her straw *petate*. "Supposedly household idols"? Supposedly discarded and given to children as dolls? Nobody knows. But it is my assumption that this was the natural sequence of events and relationships between religion and daily life throughout the world before the Industrial Revolution.

We are too rigid in our concern for precise definitions, as though the human experience were enacted in absolutes instead of in the haphazard fashion familiar to us, which we know from intimate experience to be consistently ambiguous. We must assume that the people of Teotihuacan were as gentle with their children as are the contemporary Mexicans, and that the peoples of India, Africa, Baffin Island, and the preindustrial world have retained their age-old habits. This bestows no virtue on them other than a way of life different from that of the West, whose iconography has not encouraged playing with religious figures except when they are a set of crèche figures or dolls made for children's play and religious instruction.

Perhaps the most unusual of these dolls are the ones to be found during the Christmas season, on December 23, in Oaxaca, Mexico. There, abnormally large radishes are transformed into creatures of the night for the annual fiesta called *Noche de los Rábanos* (Night of the Radishes); the radish is King of the Carnival. It is carved into human shape; the attached arms and legs, extended, have the frozen attitudes of penny woodens, but with a significant difference: their grotesque sizes and shapes evoke in the Indian imagination macabre but humorous demons and devils whose malevolence is sheer pretense.

Handcrafted dolls from the Appalachians and Ozarks are as diverse as the people who make them. Fashioned from corn shucks,[70] hickory nuts, apples, rags, stockings, wood, corncobs, and gourds, they are never coy or simpering or other than like the best examples you might have found generations ago. Simple and earthy, the materials reflect the honesty and independence of these part-time craftsmen and women. Traditions are recalled with deliberation. Variations on an old theme are subtle and slow to change. This is the art of an American people in one sector of the country where dulcimers, banjos, fiddles, and guitars accompany the ballads brought from England, Scotland, and Ireland. Country music finds new voices and new stories, but the dolls remain rooted in the past. Popular art invariably displays an exuberance of design and decoration, a delight in the grotesque, humorous observation of neighbors, a splendor of color, and, best of all, the joy of life expressed in the creative act, no matter how simple. Their aim and direction are as confident, as sure as those of the Zen archer whose bow and arrow are a natural extension of himself.[71] Man, hand, tool, and materials are as one. The rhythm of life's traditions continues only as long as there are people to repeat or weave variations on some part of the past. "Out of my own imagination and from observing costumes of the people at the turn of the century, I have originated my own style of dress for my Ozark Apple Faced Dolls. . . . I know of no other people who would have dared to combine calico with lace, yet it gave the gentility that was a part of these people and at the same time was economical."[72]

Their craft language is understood wherever craftsmen enjoy the unspoken benefits of working by hand. It is a communion that requires only the sharing of a potter's wheel or the dampening of corn shucks prior to forming them into shape. Whether the craft is that of an American Indian or women in Czechoslovakia (where they fashion for export a variety of the most intriguing corn-shuck dolls), the basic techniques are similar and unchanging. Their vocabulary eloquently expresses the traditions of mankind. This continuing, shared responsibility for preserving from destruction the handwork of the world is another kind of underground revolution.[73] What was once considered an exclusively rural occupation has in recent years become part of the urban landscape. Ironically, science and technology are bringing together widely disparate people. Before we leave the planet earth for distant worlds, we are beginning to seek out those fundamentals that have been lost or ignored. City dwellers are returning to handwork to satisfy themselves. This brings to mind the sick city cat who, to cure himself, devours the spare blades of grass thrusting up through the pavement.

I have known young people in the city who created dolls based on their own experience. Several years ago, on the Lower East Side of New York, a young woman delighted in re-creating the people she saw each day on the street: Standing Gypsy, Tanta Malka, Ukrainian Lady, Nun were some of her extraordinary character dolls. Both she and the dolls have disappeared, but another has moved into the neighborhood to take her place.

Like a celebration of fireworks, the vitality of this "melting pot" of nations often explodes in violence. Though there is little apparent beauty in these mean streets and houses, this crumbling edge of the city recalls for me the sun-baked *barrios* of Latin America. The shattered glass of abandoned automobiles covers the sidewalks, and music spills out of the doorway alongside a store window where a doll with blond braids and wistful face sits near a standing black doll with black woolen braids. Inside, at the cluttered worktable facing the

8. These two black-faced cotton dolls were found on the beach at Coney Island in Brooklyn, at the edge of the Atlantic Ocean, on a cold Sunday morning in winter. Their painted black box, shaped like a coffin, was tied with string. Inside, the dolls were wrapped in two slips of notebook paper on which was written in blue ink: "Salvador. Tomas. Miguel. Americo. Alberto. Damione." Nothing else. Rusting needles pierced the heads, arms, and bodies of these ill-fated voodoo dolls. Were they to be buried in the sand, had they been consigned to the waves, or were they intentionally left on the beach for anyone to find? Made in the United States, probably in the 1960s, they are 2¾ and 3 inches high. *Collection Leo and Dorothy Rabkin, New York City.*

street, a woman is modeling a doll's head in clay. The table is a cornucopia of smiling dolls' heads, and with the same smile of welcome the doll maker greets her visitors—two boys, a lady with a shopping bag, and myself. I am reminded of an Englishman who more than a hundred years ago recorded his observations in sympathetic and exact detail: "The making of dolls, like that of many a thing required for a mere recreation, a toy, a pastime, is often carried on amidst squalor, wretchedness, or privation, or—to use the word I have frequently heard among the poor—'pinching'. . . . A vendor of dolls expresses an opinion that as long as ever there are children from two years old to ten, there will always be purchasers of dolls; 'but for all that,' said he, 'somehow or another 'tis nothing of a trade to what it used to be. Spoiled children are our best customers. Whenever we sees a likely customer approaching—we, that is, those who know their business—always throw ourselves in the way, and spread out our dolls to the best advantage. If we hears young miss say *she will* have one, and cries for it, we are almost sure of a customer, and if we see her kick and fight a bit with the nuss-maid we are sure of a good price. If a child *cries well* we never baits our price. Most of the doll-sellers are the manufacturers of the dolls—that is, I mean, they puts 'em together. The heads are made in Hamburg; the principal places for buying them in London are at Alfred Davis's, in Hounds-ditch; White's, in Houndsditch; and Joseph's, in Leadenhall-street.' ''[74]

A century has brought profound changes in the manufacture of dolls by the poor—it exists no more. Mrs. Paula de Aragon studies sculpture at the National Academy of Design in New York City. Dolls like the ones she made for her young daughter, now grown older, are offered to a community of Italians, Jews, Poles, Ukrainians, Puerto Ricans, and Negroes in a shop whose door is always open to these neighbors. In a way she resembles the vanishing shoemaker at his last. No two of her dolls are alike, yet they all have the same endearing wistfulness of expression. They are good-humored and robust. The bodies and costumes of these long-limbed girls and boys are of printed and stuffed fabric scraps; the heads are cloth molded over clay and painted in oils or acrylics. They are portraits of the little people next door and down the street, and of the ones who flock into Mrs. de Aragon's studio-market-place. The rapport between her and the visitors is immediate and complete. Her shop is the antithesis of a factory or supermarket. She works as she talks, the ebb and flow of customers never disturbing the tenor of her conversation or her manipulation of the clay. That particular afternoon, as two boys left her shop after arranging to pick up their doll the following day, she turned to me: "As often as I call them dolls the boys call them puppets. Some of the boys tell me they want to make puppets like mine when they grow up—they think it's a 'cool' job."

This popular response to her dolls is gratifying, and it corroborates what many have argued over the years: that giving people a choice between a machine-stamped object or doll and one made by hand is the only way to educate them and to raise the standards of both young and old. The study and preservation of *now* is as important as the preservation of *then*. Perhaps it is all-important. The erosion of contemporary creativity by neglect is the common fault of people and institutions. However, the fault also lies with the producers who confine themselves to their workshops, waiting hopefully for the buyers to find them. If the popular arts of the people—and the making of dolls is one of these arts—are to survive and flourish, then it is suggested that these arts be taken to the rural and urban marketplaces of the nation. Here are the true centers of communication, of the stimulation of sight, sound, and smell, which concludes with that precious moment of decision when someone says: "I'll buy it!"

Craftsmen have long been riding out of the villages, valleys, and mountains to meet their customers and other craftsmen at craft fairs throughout the country. Their dolls are eagerly sought, and a good doll maker sells everything she makes, often on the first day of a three-day event. The dangers of isolation are no longer a threat to the individual trapped in a restricting environment. Sharing a common experience with other doll makers is like opening a door into a stranger's home. The excitement of seeing the unknown, the new, is a tangible part of the educational process. One is challenged and encouraged to change the shape of a doll's head, the movement of the body, the gesture of a hand, or the texture of the clothing. This cultural exchange is producing an American renaissance of unlimited scope and potential. More people are doing more things for their own enjoyment.[75] The absurdity of the machine's built-in obsolescence is a contradiction of the human experience. We insist on longevity. Forced disintegration of objects and people is unacceptable even to the most affluent.[76]

To rediscover our cultural roots and have the products of our digging forever housed in locked cases is no longer sufficient, nor does it answer the questions of the young who are now planting tenuous roots in country and city soil. It was suggested to me by a friend who had returned from Haight-Ashbury, San Francisco, in 1967 that we immediately collect the arts and crafts being made by the "flower children," who were then the focus of much national publicity. He was enthusiastic about what they were creating and urged that we put together a traveling exhibition that would present to the American people this sudden wild flowering. In essence, we would have been gathering the living folk arts of an urban group, which in its unprecedented coming together for a brief moment in our history would have had something to tell us about them and perhaps about ourselves. Like so many projects generated at lunch, it remained a provocative idea never realized. We will never know what was lost.

The current fragmentation of exhibits—a random case of toys, a doll in a chair, a rattle, a bonnet and dress, a doll's house—adds little but historical decoration. Other than showing dolls and antique playthings as furnishings of a vanished era that we scan with a sentimental eye, the collections do nothing more than skim the surface of the child in our world. Indeed, it is our world, for better or worse, as seen from above, from an adult's-eye view, where children resemble so many scurrying beetles. We have complacently applauded our efforts to preserve and display the history of adult man in all his glory; the time is ripe to acknowledge the existence of the child in all his stumblings to adulthood. His toys and games, dolls and paintings, inventions and constructions, dress and furniture, music and songs—all the trivia of his pockets and secret caches—demand a home of their own, a building devoted to the preservation and projection of the world of the child that would reveal strata upon strata of childhood archaeology.[77] One is reminded of the academic argument of whether to include photography among the *fine* arts. Of course, the child is older than photography; thus, he may be admitted to the hierarchy because age is equated with respectability.

The distillation of our search has not produced a guide for the perplexed. More questions than answers have been found, which is perhaps not a bad thing when dealing with a subject everyone takes for granted. Meanwhile, the roster of exhibitions and doll collectors increases, along with a scarcity of quality dolls. If the argument of this book is to be considered, the scope and content of future collections must be extended, as well as their definitions of "doll." The emphasis on the doll as a child's plaything is both misleading and confusing to collectors, curators, dealers, and everyone I consulted. Only once was I taken by surprise, and that was in a casual encounter with innocence(?) in the guise of a young man who, after learning that I was working on a doll book, said: "Like voodoo dolls?" His prompt response returned me full circle to my first instinctual thought, which suggested that the doll is best known by its associations.

There is not one doll or one criterion. Everything depends on the confluence of time and attitudes past and present. For the young man involved with the experimental attitudes of today's youth there was no doubt that his concept of the doll should also be mine. Anything that was not part of his immediate experience and was outside the realm of his rejected past was rejected because it was old. The rest of us lean gratefully on evocations of experience, no matter how laboriously we must delve to unearth our tarnished memorabilia.

My hope for the unknown "classical" doll lies in the one being created by artist-craftsmen who may not yet have commercial experience. In their studios today they are assembling from scraps, found objects, and new synthetics the doll to represent our time and culture. Nobody knows what forms and colors it will take, but I must expect that it will not be false to the spirit of man, and that it will not misrepresent man by distorting the natural and humble beauty we wish to see in Everyman.

A tiny, unpretentious book[78] no larger than my hand, with no more than a dozen pages of drawings tinted with washes of watercolor, begins its story (and ends mine):

"AND what would you like as a present from me?"
"A doll."
"But I gave you a doll last Christmas and one for your birthday!"
"Yes."
"So you want to have many dolls?"
"Yes."
"Now tell me, what sort of dolls do you like best? Small ones or big ones? Baby dolls or dolls dressed as grown-ups? Soft dolls, wooden dolls, or ..."
"Dolls, please, just dolls to love!"

PLATES 9—49

9. Our fair young sister on the left looks at us with a simple heart, not suspecting that life is beset with hazards and the several sins known only to man. Elder sister stands bemused and troubled by vague stirrings of jealousy—without reason, because jealousy needs no reason.

German bisque dolls with papier-mâché bodies, they were made about 1880 and are 23 inches high. Both wear satin with lace overskirts trimmed at the top and bottom with ruffled ribbons. The bodices have lace collars, puffed sleeves, and deep lace ruffles. Their ''at home'' caps are of lace-edged satin and are trimmed with artificial flowers. *Margaret Woodbury Strong Museum of Fascination, Pittsford, N.Y.*

11.   Paris was cajoled by Hera, Athena, and Aphrodite, the three deities who offered him power, wisdom, or beauty. He chose Aphrodite and beauty. It is easy to pass judgment on Paris's wisdom after the event, but what could the poor man have done to avoid the enmity of whichever two goddesses he scorned? We modestly suggest that discretion be our guide to harmony, and select all three of Jules Nicholas Steiner's bisque dolls. The younger generation would call this a "cop-out," but such a conclusion ignores the fate of Paris, whose intemperate decision led to his desertion of Oenone, the abduction of Helen, the siege of Troy, and his death in battle. Montaigne, who chose wisdom, wrote that "fame and tranquillity can never be bedfellows." We prefer Montaigne's bed of tranquillity. The three date from about 1880 and are about 12 inches high. *Margaret Woodbury Strong Museum of Fascination, Pittsford, N.Y.*

10.   These French Jumeau talking Bébés, from about 1895, are 23½ inches high. They have bisque heads and jointed composition bodies. The short-haired blond Bébé has obligingly removed her metal breastplate to show us that she can say "Good day, my dear little mother" and other pretty phrases from the label marked "Polichinelle." Thomas Alva Edison patented his first mechanism for a talking doll in 1878; what he released from his Pandora's box may never be undone. *Margaret Woodbury Strong Museum of Fascination, Pittsford, N.Y.*

Direotions
Sew up the sides
and head and stuff
with cotton. Cut paste
board oval to fit
bottom piece then
sew together

12. The success of Harriet Beecher Stowe's *Uncle Tom's Cabin* inspired many commercial products. Probably this cutout rag doll, patented by Celia Smith in 1893 and printed by the Arnold Print Works, was prompted by the original Topsy. The Colemans list three others named Topsy, all manufactured between 1893 and 1910. Ours is in no way similar to the other examples; her arms fall within the contours of her body, and her rounded shape makes her easy for a child to clutch. Unfortunately, the hat she holds is not a separate piece, for she would have looked most appealing in such a floppy hat. Her height is 9 inches. *Collection Margaret Whitton, Bridgewater, Conn.*

13. These painted rag-doll "Philadelphia Babies" were distributed by J. B. Sheppard of Philadelphia between 1860 and 1935, a rather long life-span for a company of which little seems to be known. Like most rag dolls, they have survived because they are of healthy stock. Their simplicity is in marked contrast to the elegance of their European cousins. There is something almost Spartan in the American dolls, something which reflects the vigor and honesty of Thoreau. "When I see a fine lady or gentleman dressed to the top of the fashion, I wonder what they would do if an earthquake should happen, or a fire suddenly break out, for they seem to have counted only on fair weather, and that things will go on smoothly and without jostling. Those curls and jewels, so nicely adjusted, expect an unusual deference from the elements."* Height, 18 inches. *Margaret Woodbury Strong Museum of Fascination, Pittsford, N.Y.*

*SELECTED JOURNALS OF HENRY DAVID THOREAU, *edited by Carl Bode. New York: New American Library, 1967, p. 51.*

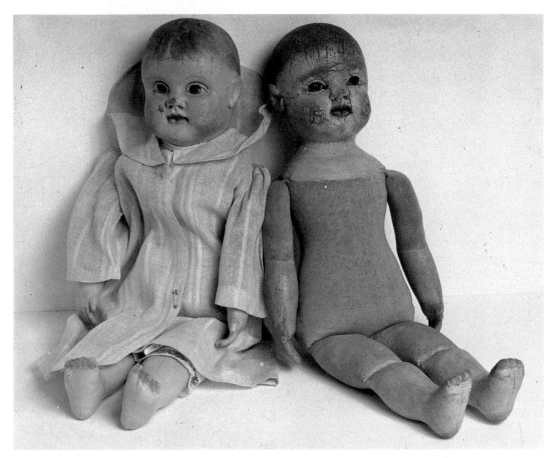

14. Her jutting chin puzzled me. I had never seen a doll's face with such aggressive character. But the mystery was solved after I discovered that her head is the bottom of a clay pipe. Her hair is painted yellow and her clay-pipe head is disguised by the elaborately frilled cap with its bright red ribbon. The legend on her apron has lost a few words:

My name is Miss Piper;
. . . pen wiper;
. . . if from your shoes
Your buttons you lose,
Just bring them to me
And directly you'll see
With what great delight
I'll sew them quite tight.

She is a sewing doll, a prop who holds the needle and thread firmly to her flat bosom. She wears a red cotton dress and white apron, and at her side is a black sewing bag large enough to hold thimble, thread, and needles. She has no arms, hands, or feet. She was made in the United States, probably in the nineteenth century, and is 8 inches high. *New-York Historical Society.*

15. Her fine calligraphic eyebrows have the clarity of a Japanese brushstroke. She is an English doll, probably of the nineteenth century, with brown eyes set into her wax-over-composition head. She is 21 inches high. Her face has cracks as fine as her unkempt hair and her nose is chipped, but her wistful smile ignores these vicissitudes. She is a good friend, and if she neglects herself it is because there are things more important than keeping her hair and kid hands well groomed. In Switzerland, where she was purchased, she was governess to a banker's child. It made no difference to her. Even when she was cast aside and flung into the closet to make way for a prettier French doll, she was confident that a good place would be found for her. She was quite right. *Collection Frances Walker.*

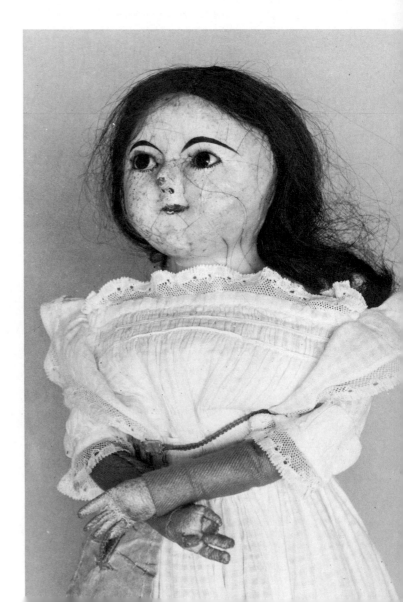

16. Meet Ethel Monticue, the breathless heroine of *The Young Visiters*. This young lady is my choice for the role, which was written at age nine by Daisy Ashford, whose observations of her Victorian elders in fact and fiction deserve to be quoted in full. Ethel, "commonly called Miss M.," is a young lady who knows what she wants. Her conduct, her poise, her responses are doll-like in their "presumshion."

Oh Bernard muttered Ethel this is so sudden.

No no cried Bernard and taking the bull by both horns he kissed her violently on her dainty face. My bride to be he murmured several times.

Ethel trembled with joy as she heard the mistick words.

Oh Bernard she said little did I ever dream of such as this and she suddenly fainted into his out stretched arms.

Oh I say gasped Bernard and laying the dainty burden on the grass he dashed to the waters edge and got a cup full of the fragrant river to pour on his true loves pallid brow.

She soon came to and looked up with a sickly smile. Take me back to the Gaierty hotel she whispered faintly.

With plesure my darling said Bernard I will just pack up our viands ere I unloose the boat.

Ethel felt better after a few drops of champagne and began to tidy her hair while Bernard packed the remains of the food. Then arm in arm they tottered to the boat.

Unable to resist quoting, but recognizing the impossibility of filling these pages with the further adventures of Miss M., I reluctantly compromise with a couple of sentences from chapter 12, "How It Ended":

Ethel and Bernard returned from their Honymoon with a son and hair a nice fat baby called Ignatius Bernard. They soon had six more children four boys and three girls and some of them were twins which was very exciting.*

Our Ethel is a German bisque made by Kestner about 1895–1900, 24 inches high, with a papier-mâché body and wooden lower arms and upper legs. *Collection Gene Moore, New York City.*

London: Chatto & Windus, 1919.

17.   This mid-nineteenth century English wax feminist has adopted the slogan of the American Revolution.
She is standing before a political banner which proclaims: WEST VINCENT DELEGATION. NO TAXATION WITHOUT
REPRESENTATION. Her impassioned lecture to the ladies of West Vincent, Pa., has suffused her face with
a hectic purple. Dressed in her best but aged silk taffeta trimmed with lace, her enamel pendant is her sole
concession to personal adornment and her ''weaker'' sex. She stands 22 inches high in her white kid high-
button shoes. *Chester County Historical Society, West Chester, Pa.*

18.   This three-breasted sweet-cookie doll from Italy is a fertility symbol. When newly baked, she had a most appetizing aroma, and one could safely say that she was good enough to eat. I was sorely tempted, but her beauty and symbolism stayed my greed. Though she has lived with us for so many years she has not aged, nor has a crumb been lost. Such dolls of dough may have had their beginnings in the baked clay idols or dolls of about 3000 B.C. found in Cyprus. The pinched clay features and ornaments, including what resemble three breasts, as well as the elaborate headdress and necklace, suggest the ancestry of today's fertility doll. Baked in 1960, she is 14¾ inches high. *Collection the author.*

19. The faces of hickory-nut dolls are more eloquent than those of many modeled and painted dolls. One must peer closely to notice this lady's tiny teeth—false, of course—and delicately sketched eyes. Her wrinkles are countless. She is quick-witted and irascible and remembers everything that has ever happened to her, her husband, and her innumerable hickory grandchildren. She is never without her shawl, which has long been molded to her body. They have always been country people. Carolyn Sherwin Bailey, in her classic *Miss Hickory*, wrote: "The tilt of her sharp little nose, her pursed mouth and her keen eyes were not those

of a doll. You and I would have known Miss Hickory as the real person that she was."* One must say the same for her husband. His garments are someone's castoffs, but what matters most to him is their warmth. Winters are hard in their part of the country. If the sleeves are too long, the better to cover his rheumatic fingers. He rarely speaks, but what is there left for him to say? They were made in the late nineteenth or early twentieth century. She is 5¼ and he is 6¼ inches high. *New-York Historical Society.*

*New York: Viking, 1946, p. 10.

21. How many ways can a doll be carved in wood? Our round-eyed, round-headed, smiling one could have been part of a Louise Nevelson construction *before* someone felt compelled to transform this found lathe-turned object into a doll. He could be a chess piece, though nothing more complicated than a pawn. He could be an idol or the body of a large rubber stamp. Instead, he is a doll.

His seated companion is painted in somber black with red trim. His face is brown and his mustache black. He is a very loose-jointed and flexible 22 inches high. Both dolls were probably made in the United States in the second half of the nineteenth century. *Margaret Woodbury Strong Museum of Fascination, Pittsford, N.Y.*

20. He still smiles beneath his scarred paint, and his bright glass eyes are not dimmed. That this primitive wooden boy doll was found in the family of a New England ship's captain, and that he was carved aboard ship sometime in the nineteenth century, may not be factually accurate, but there must have been seamen who preferred carving wooden dolls for their daughters at home to scratching away at scrimshaw—an art that has never captured my interest. He stands 13 inches high. *Margaret Woodbury Strong Museum of Fascination, Pittsford, N.Y.*

22. These rock maple dolls were made in Vermont about 1873 by Joel Ellis and his Co-operative Manufacturing Co. Ellis, like so many Yankees of his era, was an inventive genius who manufactured toys and furniture before turning to the creation of wooden dolls. He may have been influenced by the early articulated lay figures used by European artists, but his dolls are more restricted in their movements. The mortise-and-tenon joints, rigid head, and metal hands and feet in no way resemble the supple ball-jointed articulation of a lay figure, whose very fingers and toes are movable. But the lathe-turned Ellis dolls suggest the manikin and come close to being indestructible. Their heads were pressed under steam pressure and hand painted; they are 12 to 15 inches high. *Margaret Woodbury Strong Museum of Fascination, Pittsford, N.Y.*

23. Nothing is known of her origin except that she is American. I would suggest that she was made in the latter part of the nineteenth century. She has a carved wooden head and wears a false-looking white wig. Is she a portrait of the doll maker's wife, mother, grandmother? Whoever she was—and I believe she was *somebody*—there is an air of distinction about her, an independence, an authority not often seen in a doll. Hers is a strong country face, alert to the signs of the seasons. She is 12 inches high and wears a blue-and-white cotton print dress, blue-and-white checked apron, coarse apricot-colored slip, and long white pantalettes. *Essex Institute, Salem, Mass.*

24. A peg wooden doll from Germany of about 1860, 17½ inches high, with a removable fabric mask: a dull description of this beady-eyed, suspicious, potato-nosed, toothless old gossip. She stands ready to pummel with her umbrella anyone who crosses her path. Indeed, this is a character doll without equal, quite perfect in her careless disregard of appearances; her bonnet is a masterpiece of bonnets, beneath which may be seen a wig of braided rope. Across the border in Switzerland, the costume of Alti Dante (Old Auntie)—an old-fashioned dress, a bonnet, a printed cotton shawl, and an umbrella—could be seen at the Basel carnival on both men and women. Switzerland is but a stone's throw from Germany or Austria, where carnival masks were made for *Fasching* (the chasing away of winter). Alas, today the masks are plastic and have, as one would expect, a machine-produced monotony of expression. Our doll's mask may be slipped to the top of her head, revealing a pleasant-faced young peg wooden doll who wouldn't dream of hitting anyone with her umbrella. *Collection Mary Merritt, Douglassville, Pa.*

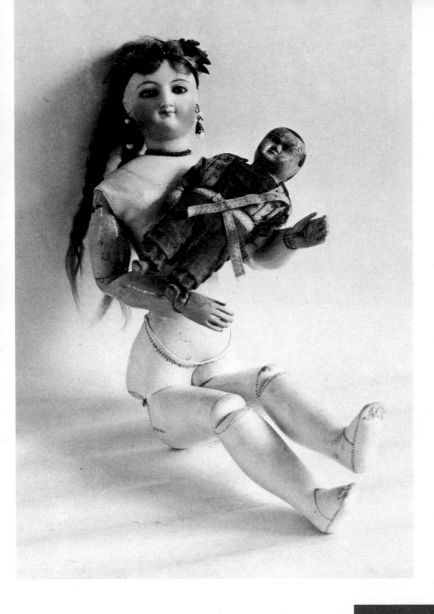

25. French, about 1875, 13 inches high, this beautifully sculptured and articulated lady has a bisque swivel head and a leather body, wooden arms and hands, blue eyes, pierced ears with earrings, blond wig with long braids, and a gilded choker. The poor little unarticulated rubber doll she has adopted is 5 inches high and was made in the United States by one of the Goodyear brothers in about 1860. He was made in a mold, and is dressed in curious decorated tan linen trousers, hand scalloped around the bottom and outer seams; his pleated blouse is of two shades of tan linen, polka-dotted in black. *Newark Museum, N.J.*

26. A doll-dressmaker's manikin, probably early eighteenth-century Flemish, she is 27 inches high. Her head is carved and painted wood, her torso is made of cork, and she stands securely on a wooden standard. An elaborate wig once covered the plain painted hair. The oversize but magnificently carved hands are an expressive reminder that this lady might have been sent by a queen or princess to a royal friend in another country, exciting admiration and perhaps envy. Her contemplative eyes look inward and she listens to other voices whispering: "Timor mortis conturbat me." *Collection Margaret D. Patterson, Sand Lake, N.Y.*

27.   A figure manipulated by means of a thread has been an amusement of many civilizations; in France the name is Pantin, in Germany Hampelmann, and in English-speaking countries Jumping Jack. Our paper Pantin was printed during the nineteenth century by the Pellerin firm, whose ''Images d'Epinal'' best represented the popular art of the French people of the eighteenth and nineteenth centuries, just as the movies and comic strips represent the popular art of our country. If assembled, our Pierette would measure 18½ inches. *Chester County Historical Society, West Chester, Pa.*

28. This English fortune-telling doll of wood and paper is from the late eighteenth century. She wears a bodice of lace over silk with a coral necklace, and her skirt is of variously colored folded papers on which fortunes are written. She has jointed wooden arms. Of the numerous wooden dolls owned by Queen Victoria, one was a fortune-telling doll, though not as pretty as this proud young lady, whose fortunes have revealed the future to girls impatient to know what lies ahead. Times change, and today the eager young, as well as the hopeful aging, turn to the pages of their newspapers and magazines for their horoscopes. Height 7½ inches. *New-York Historical Society.*

29. "Dressed to the nines!" I am hard pressed to determine whether she is well dressed, badly dressed, or simply a historical reflection of her time and place in society. Is she not just a little too elaborately finished, as though she did not know when to stop? I confess that the draped silk cording with frog closings suggests to me the treatment of a window. Her velvet brocade dress is trimmed with royal blue satin and ecru lace. I admire the panache of her royal blue plush hat with its picot-edged beige silk ribbon. One must forgive any momentary lapse in taste in one so much *une femme du monde.* On the Champs-Elysées, envious stares follow her. Who is she?

A bisque French Bru of about 1885–95, 21 inches high, she has a kid body, wooden lower limbs, bisque forearms and hands, delicately modeled ears, a fair complexion, retroussé nose, and a tendency to plumpness which will, alas, inevitably prevail in her middle years. *The Brooklyn Museum.*

30. This papier-mâché golden-haired doll's head with blue glass eyes probably comes from nineteenth-century Germany. The shape of her head and hair reminds me of a much older doll (about 1530) found recently in a Rhenish castle. Can one justifiably say that any national group retains certain physical characteristics over several centuries? A. L. Kroeber writes: "The tree of life is eternally branching, and never doing anything fundamental but branching, except for the dying away of branches."* The doll maker creates what he knows best, the people he lives with. So it was with the craftsmen who carved wooden dolls in 1530 and with those who made the first mold for this doll's head. Only the style of dress has changed. *Collection Mary Merritt, Douglassville, Pa.*

*Quoted in Clyde Kluckhohn, MIRROR FOR MAN. *New York: McGraw-Hill, and Toronto: Whittlesey House, 1949, p. 64.*

31. Two German dolls, one bisque and the other china, or the difference between a cloudy day and one resplendent with sunlight. Our bisque doll dates from about 1910, is 21 inches high, has a brown mohair wig, sleepy brown eyes, a stuffed kid body with bisque arms and hands, and legs of cloth from the knees down. Her legs, as you can see, are not helped by her striped stockings. Something disturbs her, a premonition that the years ahead will bring sadness for herself and her beloved older brothers. Luckily she escaped before 1914, but she never saw her family again. The china doll, from about 1895–1900, is also 21 inches high, has molded blond curly hair and painted blue eyes. She has never become reconciled to this century; her strict moral code belongs to the nineteenth. These two dolls have become good friends, and though they exchange pleasantries with the French dolls, there is certainly a marked coldness in the air. *New York Doll Hospital.*

32. This group portrait of the nineteenth-century French bourgeoisie shows them clean, bright, and modishly dressed in their Sunday best.

From left to right:

(1) A beautiful flirty-eyed Jumeau wears her original blond wig. The eyes open and close, and move to the left or right by means of a lever at the back of her bisque neck. She is 25 inches high.

(2) A sober, brown-eyed bisque with a jointed composition body, original from head to toe. She is 16 inches high.

(3) A Steiner Bébé with blue eyes and bisque head on a composition body. The lever which opens and closes her eyes has not been properly positioned and has left her with a vacuous, wide-eyed stare. She is 24 inches high.

(4) This long-faced original Jumeau has brown eyes, a blond wig, pierced ears, and a composition body. Even her shoes are marked "Jumeau." She was bought in Philadelphia in 1875, and she stands 24 inches high.

(5) She is a Bru. An unusual feature is her jointed wooden body; most Brus have bodies of kid or composition. She is 16 inches high.

(6) This 28-inch Jumeau is completely original, dating from 1885. She has blue eyes, a blond wig, earrings in her pierced ears, and a composition body. Her bisque complexion, like all the others', is flawless.

This sextet is truly a remarkable group. *Collection Frances Walker.*

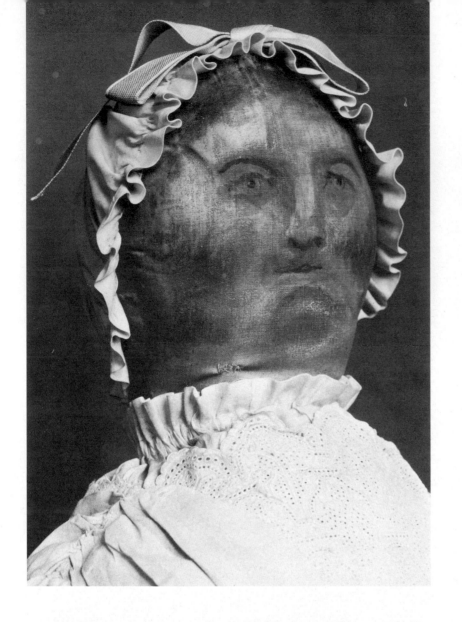

33. This rag doll with painted face, made in the United States about 1890, is a proper nanny, whose deportment can never be criticized. The children tease (rag?), but she knows they love her as she loves them. Now that they are grown, she wanders without purpose from one cold room to another. Her mistress is frugal and the heat is confined to the kitchen range. She has known few days of comfort. Who will take care of her in her old age? She is 23½ inches high. *Newark Museum, N.J.*

34. This doll has an ineffable charm and sympathy of expression. She is Queen Anne style, English, late seventeenth or early eighteenth century, 20½ inches high. Made entirely of wood except for her black glass eyes, she has a slit for hair in the top of her head and carved, painted features. Her legs are jointed at hip and knee, and her arms at shoulder and elbow. The fingers are separated. She is wearing a green silk dress decorated with flowers, sheer white cap and apron, knee-length wool stockings, and green silk slippers.

Her companion is a rag doll of unknown origin. She is probably nineteenth century, from almost anywhere in the United States. She is wearing a long brown silk cape with blue velvet collar. Her large checked bonnet is tied with an olive-green ribbon. She wears a simple polka-dotted blue cotton dress, and stands 17½ inches high. *New-York Historical Society.*

35. Someone repaired her favorite wax doll head, and her skill went undetected until I noted the roving left eye; the line of joining soon followed. The doll (the hair style suggests a boy) has inset glass eyes and is considered to be English, about 1810. Our blue-eyed young lady from France, whose silver hair tumbles from a slit in her wax head, is a Parisienne, born about 1849. If her dating is correct, she was not affected by the revolution of '48 and soon adapted to the presidency of Louis Napoleon. It is unfortunate that we will never know how she was dressed. Was her clothing influenced by Empress Eugénie? *Wenham Historical Association, Wenham, Mass.*

36. A rag doll who has been stitched and stitched again is a beloved doll. The ravages of time and affection have not marred this doll's devotion to her owners, who have dressed her as a maid in a striped cotton jumper-style dress of pink, blue, tan, and white; a bandana is tied round her head. Her immaculate white apron displays a decorated handkerchief. She wears a petticoat, drawers, and two pairs of black stockings. She has finished polishing the furniture and listens, as she does every Saturday morning, to the gardener as he sings a favorite of hers—"Tenting Tonight on the Old Camp Ground." Later she will cut him a piece of her chocolate cake. She is from the United States, about 1870, and is 14¾ inches high. *Newark Museum, N.J.*

37–38. She is an English Montanari type, 27 inche[s] high, with blond hair set into a hollow wax head. H[er] eyes, which do not close, are of blue glass. Wax le[gs] are sewn onto her cloth body. Her feet are bare. Th[e] original dress of the 1830s is a creamy taffeta trimme[d] with blue ribbon and fringe. Underneath are two she[er] white, elaborately tucked petticoats, and a knitted on[e] of white yarn in a pineapple pattern. Though I cann[ot] account for her going shoeless, she impresses m[e] with her stubborn, no-nonsense view of the world. S[he] dates from about 1835–40. *Collection Frances Walker.*

39. One of the twins has suffered more than the other, but both of them express delight at having their picture taken. Of course they are dressed alike, in orange-and-white print dresses with lace trim at neck and sleeves, and printed velvet jackets of green, orange, and red. They wear plain white slips, scallop-edged pan-talettes, openwork socks with lace edges, and leather shoes. The broad-brimmed hats on their papier-mâché heads are trimmed with ribbons tying under the chin. The kid arms appear abnormally long but are not offen-sive. The dolls date from about 1850 and are 23½ inches high. Their provenance is unknown. *Essex Institute, Salem, Mass.*

WILL BE PUBLISHED, SIX KINDS.

PARLOR AMUSEMENT FOR GIRLS.

THE BRIDE.

PAPER DOLL'S.

NUMBER ONE.

McLOUGHLIN BROTHERS, Publishers, 24 Beekman St., New York.

Entered according to Act of Congress, in the year 1857, by McLOUGHLIN BROTHERS, in the Clerk's Office of the District Court of the United States, for the Southern District of New York.

40.   This is the envelope that contained a paper doll and her five costumes. The doll—in white underclothing and with arms crossed demurely over her bosom—and her trousseau are wood engravings, hand-colored front and back. Though McLoughlin Brothers proudly offer six kinds, it is believed that only four subjects were printed for the "parlor amusement" of young people throughout the United States. The Bride, 5⅛ inches high, was the first. The others were: *The American Lady with Something to Wear; Little Emma, the American Lady's Daughter;* and *Little Mary. Chester County Historical Society, West Chester, Pa.*

41.   AUTO-PERI-PA-TET-IKOS. The word is sheer necromancy. If the witches of *Macbeth* had solemnly intoned it over their cauldron, no one need have been surprised. But the real sorcery is in the key, which is for winding and setting in motion this American walking doll (patented 1862). Her metal legs and body are covered with a pink striped hoopskirt and green velvet top, both trimmed with lace. Her height is 9¾ inches. The original box is an innocent, early example of soft-sell advertising. I admire the typeface, the generous areas of empty space, and the awkward but accurate engraving, of the kind which could be enjoyed in the old weeklies before photography eliminated the need for wood engravings. *Essex-Institute, Salem, Mass.*

42. I hope these four wooden dolls from Africa will lead those doll collectors not already familiar with African art to seek out its sculpture. Certainly it is difficult to relate them to the dolls of Europe and America. They were not made for sale, or to be housed in a museum or a private collection. They are not decorative objects. Their meanings, often obscure to us, are bound up in the spiritual and social core of the people who made them, and only now are we beginning to understand this language of form and content that is so alien to everything we have known in the civilizations of East and West.

Ibeji, who created twins, is one of six hundred gods of the Yoruba pantheon. This contemporary Ibeji doll (left) is a superb example of the Nigerian carver. She is 19½ inches high, and is adorned with glass beads made in Bida, Nigeria. *Collection June Henneberger, New York City.*

The Ibibio people, who made the second doll from the left, live west of the Cross River in southeastern Nigeria. The figure bears a striking though coincidental resemblance to Chinese art, and was created within the past fifty years. Height is 9 inches.

Nothing is known about the doll (second from right) of the Bagirmi people, who live in the southeast Lake Chad region. Until very recently, these dolls were believed to come from the western Sudan. Our doll is a masterpiece of the symbolic forms and abstract shapes that so strongly influenced French art in the early twentieth century. It stands a scant 9 inches high.

A doll comparable to the one on the far right is in the collection of the British Museum, which acquired it in 1909 from the capital of the Bakuba tribe in the Congo. Height is 9½ inches. *Collection Mr. and Mrs. Irwin Hersey, New York City.*

43. These male and female carved wooden puppets from Ceylon, probably late nineteenth century, have indeed seen better days. Much of their heavy gesso has crumbled and reveals the basic wood structure beneath; on their well-articulated arms and legs the gesso has been built up as much as one-sixteenth of an inch. His carved wooden turban still shows faint traces of its once-golden splendor. Puppets from India are found in some abundance, but these are the only Sinhalese ones we were able to find. Their clothing is tattered and poor; little of their former glory remains. They are about 19 inches high. *Collection Louis F. Simon, New York City.*

44. During a luncheon, I asked the man seated on my right what he collected, since everyone else at the table collected something, mostly paintings and sculpture. He replied that he collected antique bells. And I? A few dolls. "Then you must see my dolls from Nubia, which I picked up on the Nile in 1927." Standing 8¾ and 9¼ inches tall, the dolls are covered with a multitude of glass beads (Czechoslovakian?) and dangle paper-thin coins. Why are their faces white, rather than brown or black? Was it because the doll maker had no other material on hand, or was he depicting the affluent white tourists? *Collection Nathaniel Spear, Jr.*

45. At first glance the carefully mapped lines resemble the routes on a subway map. I was familiar with the "medicine doll" called the "doctor's lady": carved in hardwood or ivory, she leans voluptuously on one elbow, apparently waiting for someone, though it is difficult to believe it is only her doctor. But I had never seen the figure used in the practice of *hari-ryoji*, or acupuncture. Made in Japan about 1880, this 26-inch papier-mâché anatomical doll maps the nervous system of man, showing the 660 spots controlling the nerves and muscles, according to that theory. I remembered an exhibition I had seen some years ago at Asia House in New York. Did I know then that I would have need of the catalogue, on a subject in which I had no interest? I turned to my bookshelf and to *Chinese Medicine: An Exhibition Illustrating the Traditional System of Medicine of the Chinese People*, that system "known as *Acupuncture*, a procedure which involves inserting into the skin a number of fine needles at precise points on the body indicated by charts worked out through the ages by some of the most famous medical authorities. Each particular group or series of points, following a given line over the body's surface, is connected with a corresponding visceral organ, and gives access, as it were, to the treatment of that organ by remote control; one being for the heart, another for the lungs, and so on.... No one has yet produced a satisfactory scientific explanation of why the Chinese use it or how it can bring about the cure of any disease.... In any case *Acupuncture* is the most remarkable feature of Chinese therapeutics." Or Japanese. *Peabody Museum, Salem, Mass.*

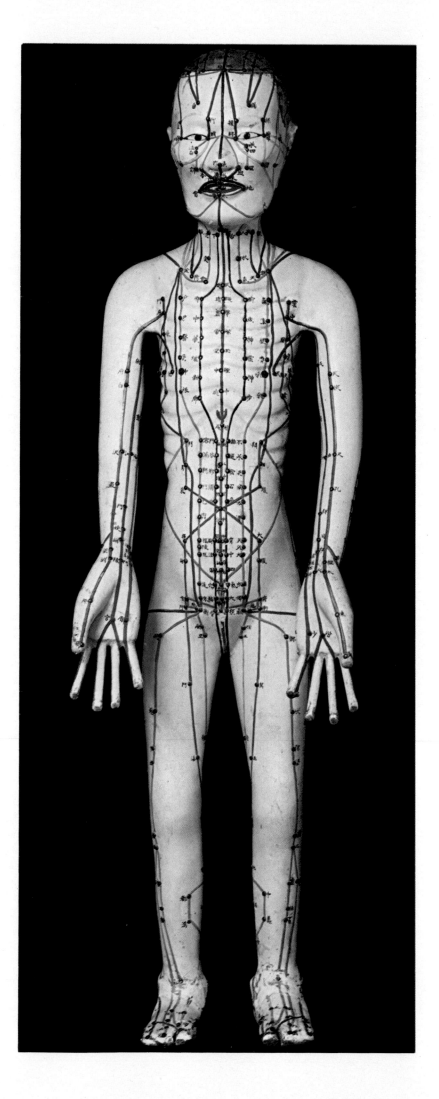

46. The traditional folk dolls of Japan reflect the life, religion, and cultural history of the Japanese people. Each doll, however humble, has its meaningful story. In our family of folk dolls, the slender two on the left, from Kurayoshi in Tottori prefecture, are called Hakata, which is said to mean locally "unsophisticated girl." They were among my first folk toys from Japan. The other four are Hoko-san, or servant, dolls, and are from the district of Shikoku, the smallest of Japan's four main islands. The Hoko-san dolls were used to cure children of "incurable" illness. They were placed in bed overnight beside the sick child, and the next morning consigned to the ocean, where they and the sickness soon vanished. All of the dolls pictured are papier-mâché, all without arms or legs. Dating from about 1950–60, they range from 3 to 5¾ inches in height. *Collection the author.*

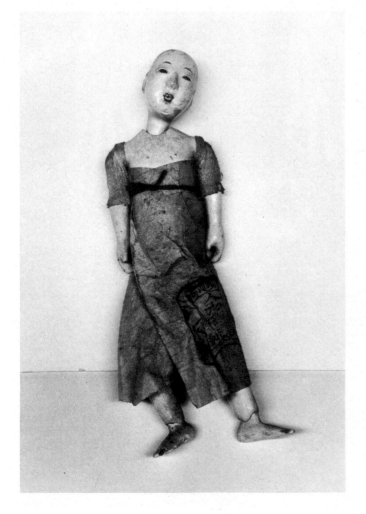

47. She is bereft of the collection of fifteen assorted wigs that always accompany her. Clad in costume and properly bewigged, this Japanese doll is transformed into a fetching beauty, but I like her just as she stands, relaxed against a wall, without pretense, even a little coarse. Made about 1915, her height is 9 inches.

An inferior version is still manufactured today, along with a box of wigs; it can be found in almost any Japanese gift shop. *Peabody Museum, Salem, Mass.*

48. These two friendly ladies from Japan, born about 1890, have seen better days. Yet they have no complaints. Their lives have been hard, but haven't the lives of the humble always been hard? Their kimonos are crude flowered block prints in large patterns. Their wooden heads are covered with *gofun*—pulverized oyster shell—and their inset glass eyes are painted with ink. The illusion that these dolls are lifesize is a tribute to the artistry of even the simplest creation of the Meiji period (1869–1912). The elaborate production that went into the making and finishing of a doll's head is best described by Tokubee Yamada in his book *Japanese Dolls,* published by the Japan Travel Bureau in 1959. These stand 6½ and 5¼ inches high. *Courtesy of the Wenham Historical Association, Wenham, Mass.*

49.   Their silk-embroidered garments may not be as lustrous as they were 150 years ago; their faces are faintly freckled and stained. However, these dolls of the Edo period (1615–1868) have a beauty I find irresistible, not only in the detailed perfection of the costume but in the sensitive modeling of each doll's face, in their purity, the poetry of restraint. Even the ears are acutely observed and modeled, revealing a sculptural quality rarely seen in a doll. There are no shortcuts in craftsmanship. The cumulative effect is like the sound of a bronze bell which one continues to hear long after the tolling has ceased. Our three court nobles are 12 inches high. *Collection Louis F. Simon, New York City.*

PLATES 50—70

50.   The empress Jingu, a legendary figure celebrated for her valor, was made by the doll craftsman Ohki about 1900 for the Boys' Festival Day, which was begun during the Edo period (1615–1868). Her garments are not embroidered and her teeth are painted black, a detail the camera does not show. The ears are abstract shapes, her quizzical expression the result of plucked eyebrows replaced by light gray touches high on the forehead. I find her face, figure, and trappings symbolic of all Japanese dolls. She is 20 inches high.

Though much has been lost and doll makers are few, what other country can boast of craftsmen who are designated "Living National Treasures"? Such a man is the contemporary doll maker Juzo Kagoshima; another is Goyo Hirata, whose Ukiyo-e dolls are based on the wood-block prints of the eighteenth and nineteenth centuries; and there is also Miss Ryujo Hori, maker of costume dolls.* Today, Japan's "Living Treasures" embrace weavers, sword smiths, dyers, ceramists, stencil makers, and lacquer artists, the traditional craftsmen of a craft-producing country, surviving stubbornly in a land where experts predict the largest industrial production in the world. *Collection Louis F. Simon, New York City.*

*See Masataka Ogawa, THE ENDURING CRAFTS OF JAPAN. *New York: J. Weatherhill, 1968.*

51.   Purchased in Shanghai in 1910, these male and female mourning dolls have carved wooden heads and stuffed bodies, arms, and legs; they are 12½ inches high. Their white robes are covered with straw netting. He wears violet trousers, hers are blue. Our search for Chinese dolls had turned up numerous traditional operatic dolls, but none were such eloquent spokesmen for the Chinese people: in their sensitive features are mirrored the great Chinese civilizations of the past. *Peabody Museum, Salem, Mass.*

52.   These two Japanese paper dolls, with their abstract shapes and colors, are a version of the Elder Sister dolls that have been made throughout Japan and which derive from votive figures associated with Girls' Day. They are made of folded paper, and were intended to teach little girls the proper use of traditional dress and cosmetics, on the realistic assumption that even the littlest girls are passionately interested in such things. Our dolls were made prior to World War I.   Both are 11 inches high. *Peabody Museum, Salem, Mass.*

53. This Eskimo doll from Nome, Alaska, of about 1935, is wearing plaid gingham ornamented with orange and purple worsted and edged with brown fur. The same fur circles her finely carved wooden face, which has painted eyes and eyebrows and black tattoo stripes on the chin. Her brown-and-black fur-topped mukluks are trimmed with white feathers plus more of the worsted. Obviously she has made good use of the trading post for her colorful attire. She is 17½ inches high, and holds in her left arm a 6-inch Eskimo doll with a carved ivory face. The little one is dressed in brown fur. *Peabody Museum, Salem, Mass.*

54. An impressive display of fine beadwork is presented in this 9-inch-long cradleboard with a rag doll, which a Sioux Indian mother made for her child in about 1890. In spite of the voluminous literature on the American Indians, few people thought enough of the children's playthings to write about them at a time when the Plains Indians were still making dolls for their children instead of buying them. Now it is too late, and few collections include Indian dolls.

The Blackfoot Indian doll is dressed in buckskin and beads and has a featureless rag face. When features were depicted, they were without individual characterization: eyes, nose, and mouth were indicated but not emphasized. About 1875, 10 inches high. *Museum of the American Indian, Heye Foundation, New York City.*

55. Our Salish Indian doll from the Pacific Northwest dates from about 1900 and is 18 inches high. The wooden cradle and the baby in high relief are both carved from the same piece of wood, a fine example of the Northwest Indians' genius as wood sculptors. "The [Indian baby] spent the first year of his life on a cradleboard. This was the case with all American Indians ... some [cradleboards] were made of basketry, some of wood. Northwesterners preferred their favorite cedar wood. They used a section of slender trunk and hollowed it out.... Then they filled it with shredded cedar bark. In this, the naked baby was bedded as carefully as a jewel in cotton."* Our doll in swaddling clothes has no arms. He may have been a model for young mothers and children in the art of swaddling an infant properly. *Museum of the American Indian, Heye Foundation, New York City.*

*Ruth Underhill, INDIANS OF THE PACIFIC NORTHWEST. *Washington, D.C.: Bureau of Indian Affairs, 1944, p. 128.*

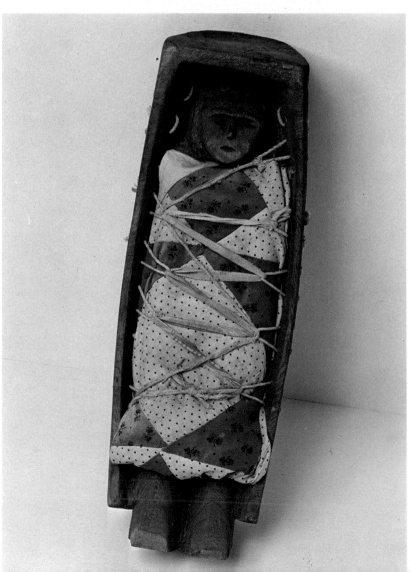

56. From left to right:

(1) The Blackfoot Indian doll from western Canada, made in about 1840–50, has a carved wooden head with inlaid pearl-button eyes and wears buckskin clothing. He was not a child's plaything but was probably used as a fetish or charm. The Blackfoot are an Algonquian tribe and are remembered as being among the fiercest of Plains warriors. I find this doll anything but aggressive; his attitude is benign and disarming. He is 16 inches high.

(2) This Blackfoot Plains Indian doll of about 1875, 14 inches high, is beautifully attired. The elegant simplicity of her dress and its striking design make it a classic which might have come from the studios of designers Bonnie Cashin, Pauline Trigere, or Norman Norell. She is one of the most sophisticated of the Indian dolls, so unlike her buckskin sisters. Though her wooden head is sensitively carved, it is her costume that places her, for me, in the tradition of French fashion dolls.

(3) The Sioux Indian doll represents a "ghost dancer"; the painted thunderbird on his shirt is common to the Indians who participated in the dance, "accompanied by certain songs, which the prophet [a Paiute Indian of Nevada] claimed would eventually cause the disappearance of the whites, bring back the dead Indian peoples, and restore the buffalo and old ways of life on the Plains."* His braided hair is real; he wears buckskin clothing and beaded moccasins. The Sioux put up a brave fight against the United States Army at Wounded Knee, South Dakota, in 1890. Was our doll made by one of the few who lived to tell the story to their children? He is 12 inches high.

(4) This Crow Indian doll, made in the 1890s, is dressed in buckskin and adorned by a pendant of porcupine quills. He appears to have enjoyed, or suffered from, much play. One cannot help linking this doll with an Indian child whose family and way of life had by 1890 been irreparably damaged by the migration of the whites and their systematic extermination of the Indian. The story is an inescapable part of our history, one we are loath to confront. This doll is an eloquent spokesman for a silent American minority. He is 14 inches high.

(5) Dressed in buckskin and fringed leggings, this Sioux Indian doll has real braided hair, beaded eyes and mouth. This is not the Indian painted by Remington in the nineteenth century, nor is it the heroic, lifesize wooden cigar-store Indian of my childhood. The warrior Sioux is here reduced to a solemn, uncomplaining companion, the simplest of stuffed playthings. He dates from about the 1890s and is 16 inches high.

(6) This Blackfoot Indian doll on horseback is a symbolic rider on a symbolic horse, both of them faceless, both poised for movement. The doll has strapped to his back an empty rifle or bow quiver. Gone are the buffalo and other game he once hunted from his horse, but our rider faces the future expectantly. What does he see replacing our mobile house on wheels, which has replaced his mobile tepee? He is from about the 1890s and is 9 inches high. *Museum of the American Indian, Heye Foundation, New York City.*

Alvin M. Josephy, Jr., THE INDIAN HERITAGE OF AMERICA. *New York: Alfred A. Knopf, 1969, p. 285.*

57. A Cheyenne Indian doll, of about 1850–80, 15½ inches high, she wears a costume of buckskin and beads, with elaborately beaded leggings and moccasins. Her head is of stone; her hair has all but vanished. She could have been made even while Chief Crazy Horse and Sitting Bull, with their Cheyenne and Sioux warriors, defeated Custer at Little Bighorn in 1876. Today the Cheyenne live in Montana and Oklahoma. *Museum of the American Indian, Heye Foundation, New York City.*

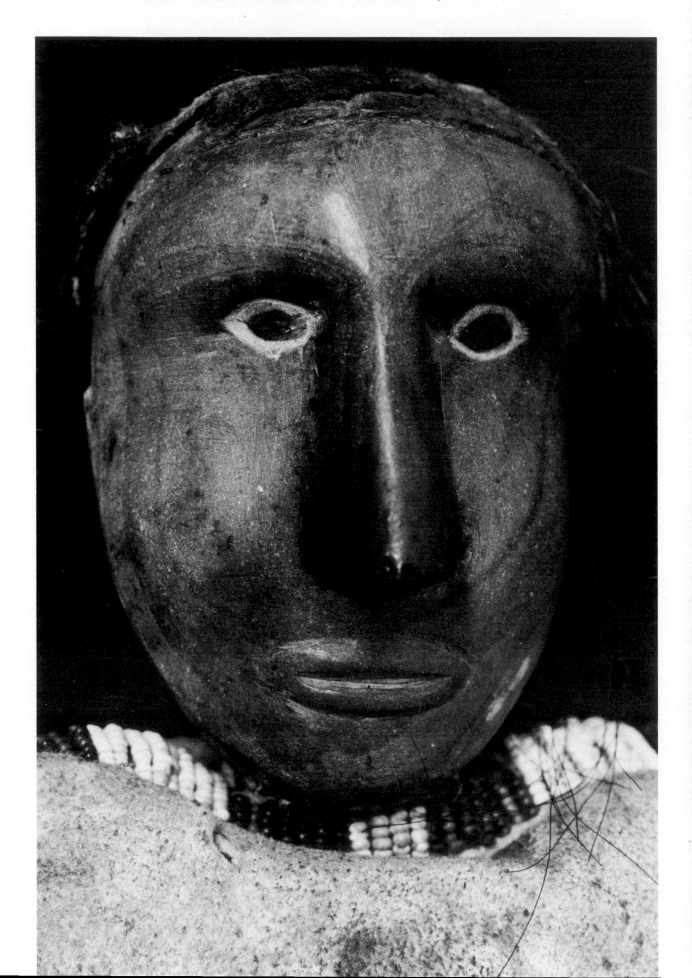

58. This Mojave Indian terra-cotta baby doll of about 1890–1910, 16 inches high, is bound in juniper fiber and wrapped with a woven yarn cradle band. Though the Mojaves live in one of the hottest regions of the United States, tradition demands the wrapping of a baby in its cradleboard whatever the temperature. Terra-cotta dolls with painted tattooing are still being made by the Mojaves, and look very much like these older examples. *Museum of the American Indian, Heye Foundation, New York City.*

59. These Apache Indian dolls, from the 1860s, wear replicas of traditional adult costumes. The dangling metal decorations must have made a sound like the one that Edgar Allan Poe called a tintinnabulation. The white man's "civilizing" influence appears timidly below the buckskin. Height 16 inches. *Museum of the American Indian, Heye Foundation, New York City.*

60. The snake dancer, at far left, is not a kachina doll. For years it was considered improper for a Hopi carver to fashion these dolls for anyone other than his own people. It is made of cottonwood, as is the snake, which is broken. It dates from about 1920 and is 10 inches high.

The other four dolls are Hopi kachinas. Colton writes: "It is difficult to find any constant character that will distinguish Hopi from Zuñi kachina dolls.... It is a general rule that the Zuñi dolls are taller and thinner.

Heheya-aumutaqa Kachina, or Heheya's Uncle, of about the 1920s, is 9 inches high. He is made in numerous variations, but his basic characteristic is a white mask with vertical zigzags. He wears a breechclout.

Polik Mana (Butterfly) Kachina, about 1910, is 14 inches high. I find the changes that have been rung on the design of this kachina most exciting. She wears her *tableta* with the dignity born of her assured role in the Hopi community. This is a noble carving.

Masao Kachin-mana Kachina, about 1900, is 7½ inches high. I suppose the older kachina dolls are easier to love, and I also find this one, along with the Butterfly Kachina to her right, a profound expression of the Indian spirit. She has a white face mask with carved wooden nose, realistic painted eyes, and hair in maiden's whorls. She wears the woman's wedding costume. It is believed that she will bring much rain.

Heheya-aumutaqa Kachina, or Heheya's Uncle, of about the 1920s, is 9 inches high. The covering of lamb's wool is still another variation. *Collection Jay-Ehret Mahoney.*

Harold S. Colton, HOPI KACHINA DOLLS. Albuquerque: University of New Mexico Press, 1949, p. 90.

61. The buckskin visitor on the far right is a long way from home; she is a 9-inch Sioux doll with papoose. The other five are Mojave Indian terra-cotta dolls ranging in height from 5 to 8 inches. The doll on the pedestal has lost her skirt, but her ornate beaded collar more than compensates for this loss. The tattooed Mojave dolls with outstretched arms and eyes uplifted bear each other a striking stylistic resemblance, suggesting they were made by the same person. The Mojave Indian doll lying in a cradleboard is daydreaming; to the Mojaves, dreams are of the utmost significance, for they are believed to foretell the future. All these dolls date from about 1890–1910. *Museum of the American Indian, Heye Foundation, New York City.*

62. The museum label for this doll of the Lenni-Lenape (also called the Delaware Indians) states: "The Odas spirit-being has power to protect the owner's health, in return for which it must be given a dance and new clothes every spring. The owner calls it his 'Grandmother.'" This doll dates from about 1850 and is 9 inches high. She has a faceless, corn-shuck head, myriad tiny beads, silver dangles, and circular metal decorations.

The Menomini Indian doll dates from about 1860 and is 7 inches high. Of Algonquian stock, this tribe was called "Wild Rice Men" by the Chippewa Indians. They have lived in Wisconsin since prehistoric times. The doll has a wooden head and body, and the costume is decorated with tiny shells and beads. *Museum of the American Indian, Heye Foundation, New York City.*

63. These Zuñi kachina dolls date from about 191
20 and are all between 13 and 14 inches high. Th
are as fine as any of the Hopi kachinas. Indeed, so
collectors find their fullness of style more satisfyi
than the comparative austerity of the Hopi dolls. I
one knows when the first kachina dolls were made
either the Hopi or Zuñi. Dockstader traces them ba
to 1850.* Perhaps the first exhibition of Indian a
and crafts to be seen by the American public was
the World's Columbian Exposition in Chicago,
1893. Private collecting began later. *Museum of*
American Indian, Heye Foundation, New York City.

*THE KACHINA AND THE WHITE MAN. *Bloomfield Hi*
Mich.: Cranbrook Institute of Science, 1954.

64. Hano (Clown) Kachina, or Koshare, on the l
is 23 inches high. A new variation on an abst
mask, this face is realistic, with an alert express
and teeth showing; only the painted lines around
eyes and mouth suggest the clown—much like
painted face of a circus clown. The extended ar
deviating so from the formal structure of the older
chinas, and the form of the fingers make this Hopi
china an unusual example of Indian realism. (
knows he is soon to begin his dance, to clown for
Indians as well as for visiting tourists.

The center doll, a Hopi representation of a Nav
dancer, is 13 inches high. I complained to Mr. I
honey that I could not find him in Colton, and he
plied that there are a number which Colton does
describe. "Unfortunately," he said, "Colton, as v
any such student, was often given false informati
This is probably true as well of those who may c
cize Colton." Honestly spoken. Let the student of
dian kachinas beware!

Ho-ó-te, or Ahote, a Hopi kachina, is 21 inc
high. This carving is typical of some done in the
fifties for the commercial trade: the once-simple h
becomes a demonstration of bravura design. The tr
tional black case mask, popeyes, snout, painted st
ruff, kilt, and sash are all there. When dancing,
would carry a rattle, bow, and arrows. All these d
are probably from the 1950s. *Collection Jay-Ehret I*
honey.

65.   These five Zuñi Indian kachina dolls were carved from the roots of cottonwood trees. Unlike the new kachinas, which are decorated with commercial tempera paints, the older ones were painted with earth colors. Most collectors refer to Harold S. Colton's book *Hopi Kachina Dolls*, which also includes the kachinas of the Zuñis, for identification of approximately 266 dolls.

   From left to right:

   (1) Kwasus Alektaqa Kachina, about 1920, height 13 inches.

   (2) Tawa Koyung, or Peacock (Sun Turkey), Kachina, about 1920, height 15 inches.

   (3) Salako, or Shalako, Kachina, probably early 1900s, height 17 inches. Because he is damaged, he has no *tableta*.

   (4) Heheya Kachina, old but of no confirmed date, height 14 inches.

   (5) Salimopiya Kachina, old but of no confirmed date, height 14 inches. Missing from his hands are his yucca-leaf whip and his bow and arrows. *Collection Jay-Ehret Mahoney.*

66. An Araucanian Indian doll from southern Chile, he was made of animal skin about 1900–1910. Together with his horse, he is 10 inches high. He sits atop woolen blankets—his people are known for their skill in weaving them. The doll is a mere suggestion of beaded head and arms, with a flat metal disk hat and cotton clothing. He is an appropriate symbol of an Indian people who, like the Seminoles, have never been conquered by force. The Spaniards gave the Araucanians their name, which means "unsubdued Indians." *Museum of the American Indian, Heye Foundation, New York City.*

67. These Mojave Indian terra-cotta dolls of about 1890–1910 are from 4½ to 6 inches high. The two hair-pulling young women are fighting over the young man who is judiciously standing aside, keeping his own counsel. The standing woman and the mother suckling her children are married and unconcerned. The museum label states: "Southwest Desert Dwellers are related to the Yuma in language and culture; sharing a similar physical build and character, they have lived in the same desert region, occupying land along the Colorado River just north of the Yuma territory. They were known for their tattooing, an art now obsolete." *Museum of the American Indian, Heye Foundation, New York City.*

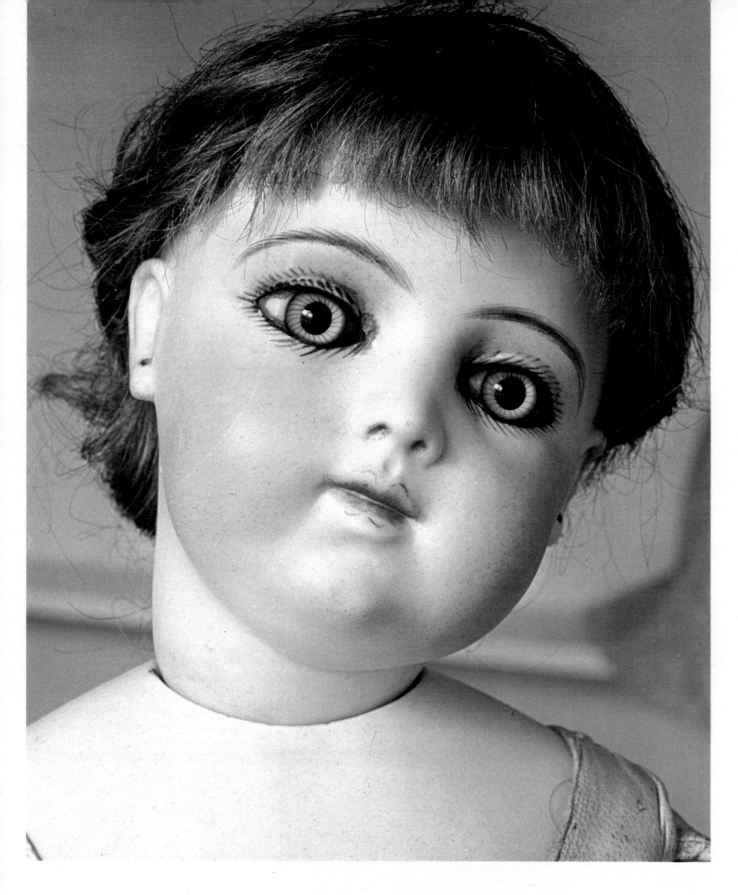

68. The quintessence of wide-eyed innocence, she is bisque, French, from about 1882, and has glass eyes, swivel neck, bisque hands, and kid body. Her height is 17 inches. Our Bru is too good to be true. If she were a child I would avoid her; as a doll she belongs in that never-neverland created by adults whose dream children live in Graustarkian palaces. If I am unduly harsh, my censure is directed not at her but at the continuing wide-eyed examples which proliferate at each holiday season. Bru's reputation is secure; since 1866, his dolls have made their way in the world. *Collection Margaret D. Patterson, Sand Lake, N.Y.*

69. A doll hospital is anything but antiseptic. Overhead hang rows of dolls' bodies. Boxes overflow with legs and arms, stockings and hats. Drawers are filled with myriad eyes—"American" eyes of plastic, glass, tin; glass "French" eyes, oval and round—and "German" hands of papier-mâché, wood, bisque, china, and kidskin. The worktable is covered with dolls in the process of rehabilitation. It is the backstage rehearsal room for a pantomime whose current attraction is this French bisque Steiner, a mechanical kicking and crying doll of about 1885. Her uncombed hair, amazed eyes, and sharp, widely spaced teeth suggest that she is playing one of the ill-fated brides of Bluebeard. *New York Doll Hospital.*

70. Does anyone remember the paintings of round-eyed children that were so popular a few years ago? Their influence spread throughout the United States, Europe, and Mexico, and prompted my special *bête noire*—Dayglo painting on velvet! How hypnotic were those eyes and, happily, how brief their success! This bisque French Jumeau of about 1895, with human hair, is a radiant beauty but—is it the near-meeting of the eyebrows that gives her an owlish look? Were such excessive brows and lashes an ideal of French womanly beauty? Standing in the shadow of our refulgent doll is a demure and pensive bisque Jumeau of about 1875–80, who, unlike her younger sister, is content to hold her tongue. *New York Doll Hospital.*

PLATES 71—106

71. Another wide-eyed young lady here tries to capture us with her enormous gaze. She is so intent upon what she is looking at that I am sure she is unaware of the unusual design her lipstick made this morning. She is bisque, perhaps French, and probably dates from the late nineteenth century. *Margaret Woodbury Strong Museum of Fascination, Pittsford, N.Y.*

72. She is waiting for Mr. Irving Chais to cover her with a cork crown prior to applying a new mohair wig. There are two wigs on forms: a blond one with metal curlers and a brunette one already curled. She has not yet made up her mind. I believe she is distracted by the dozens of boxes on the floor, piled almost to the ceiling and filled to overflowing with dolls' parts. Though it is anything but tidy within the confines of this overcrowded workroom, the miracle of rebirth goes on day after day. Brushes, bottles of flesh-colored paint, cleaners, talc, glues, shampoo—all are basic equipment for a man who has repaired thousands of dolls in the past twenty-five years. But what will happen in the next generation when our bisque Jumeau is once again in need of repairs? Will there be a craftsman to take her in? Or will all craftsmen have vanished by the year 2000? She has a papier-mâché body, stands 33 inches high, and dates from about 1895. *New York Doll Hospital.*

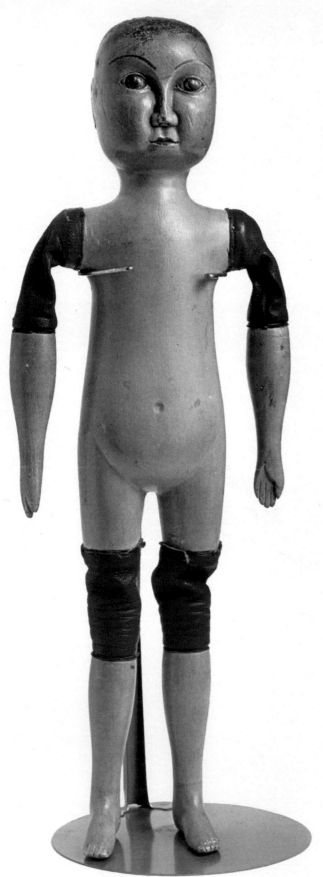

73. A sophisticated primitive wooden doll with jointed red leather arms and legs, it was made in the United States, probably in the nineteenth century. It is an enigma, daring us to guess its origin, age, and sex. I am teased by a faint recollection of another such doll somewhere among the thousands we visited. Has anyone else seen a duplicate? It is anything but a blockhead. There is intelligence in those painted blue eyes; the absence of a chin does not weaken its forceful character, its lurking sense of humor. I have decided that he was a publisher or the editor of a small country newspaper. I would have trusted him in either enterprise. He is 21 inches high. *Margaret Woodbury Strong Museum of Fascination, Pittsford, N.Y.*

74. These English peddler dolls, peripatetic saleswomen of household items, whose costume traditionally was a bonnet, wool cape, and simplest of dresses, hawked their wares in baskets or trays through city streets, country lanes, and English fairs. The profusion of trivia, as well as necessities, which they carried year in and year out must have been an endless source of fascination to remote villagers and even to city dwellers, who could stay a moment to poke about the "cornucopia" while exchanging gossip. The fetching wooden lady on the left is 7½ inches high. She has not had a successful day. It is late, but she has decided not to move along until she makes one more sale. Her bright-eyed competitor is lighting her own way in the darkening night. Her voice can be heard indoors, but the diners behind locked windows pay little heed to her street cries. She, too, is 7½ inches high, but she is made of leather with black bead eyes. Both dolls date from about 1830. *Collection Mary Merritt, Douglassville, Pa.*

75. She is a happier French cousin of our Parisian walkers, though no less impoverished. Recently arrived from the provinces, she has wandered into the museum and is delighted with the paintings and the well-dressed visitors. Her taste is uncertain and unformed, and she has hastily put together a grab bag of bodice, skirt, and underskirt. Her triumph is a paper hat whose green cloth brim sweeps upward, revealing just enough of her eyes. The hat is trimmed in gold with a green bow and, out of sight, an orchid-pink feather. Wooden, without proper arms, she stands 10 inches high and is dated 1812. *Essex Institute, Salem, Mass.*

76. Such is the skill of the photographer that he can increase to monumental size a doll just 4¾ inches high. I suppose this is what may be called camera magic. Our rag doll is homely (in the kindest sense), with softly painted features and hair, an oblong stuffed cotton body, and blue eyes to match her flowered dress. She is every child's mother, sympathetic and understanding. She is contemporary and was made in the United States. *Collection Leo and Dorothy Rabkin, New York City.*

77. Even in undress he is the very model of a modern major general—General Stark, who might have inspired the British saying that "old soldiers never die; they just fade away." Stark faded away at age ninety-four, after a vigorous military life with Rogers' Rangers in the Seven Years' War, the Battle of Bunker Hill, the defeat of Burgoyne's detachments at Bennington, Vermont, and the skirmishes around Saratoga. No wonder a grateful patriot patterned a doll for his young family after the general. One must visualize him resplendent in uniform, saber held aloft, astride a horse, his short legs pointed forward. A brave figure of a doll, although the carving of the head is rude and somewhat bluntly defined. His provenance and dates are unknown. Shall we say early nineteenth century? He is 9¾ inches high. *Essex Institute, Salem, Mass.*

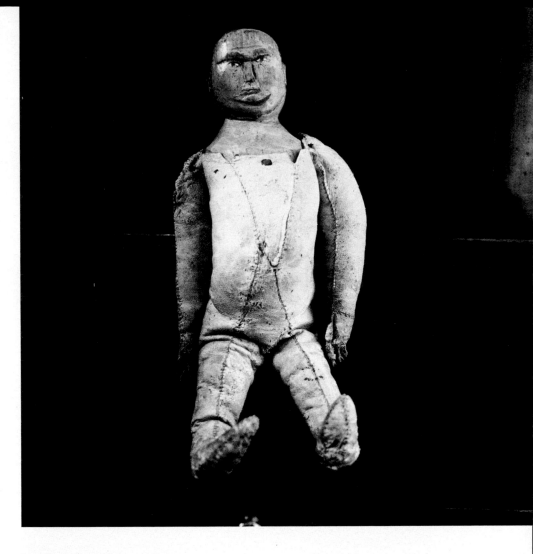

78. Our French wax doll of about 1875 emerges from her papier-mâché eggshell, not unlike Botticelli's Venus rising full-grown from her seashell. Or she might be part of the fascinating world of Hieronymus Bosch. In his painting *The Garden of Delights*, there is a man who looks backward at his own broken shell, which is already filled by a crowd of smaller figures— the next generation? Our plump-armed wax baby is a strange conceit, but she grows less strange after we contemplate the world of Bosch. Aren't children hatched just this way, and fully clothed too? She is 4 inches high. *Margaret Woodbury Strong Museum of Fascination, Pittsford, N.Y.*

79. This brown-eyed family of china dolls displays various molded hair styles. Father, who stands 21 inches high, has dark brown hair rather than the traditional black. His unmarried daughter, far left, is 22 inches high; his wife, a matronly 19 inches, has a handmade cloth body and brown kid arms. The only married daughter, who would not remove her hat, is 21 inches high. The younger daughters are, respectively, 21½ inches, 20 inches, and 17½ inches high. The seated daughter is 17 inches; the child in her arms is 10 inches. Lastly, the tiny-headed girl stands 11 inches high; she is the proud gentleman's only grandchild, small for her age. They are German, probably nineteenth century. *Collection Frances Walker.*

80. Rag Nellie is 14 inches high and was made in 1878 by Phoebe Wilson of Newark, New Jersey. Her head and hands are of white cotton stockinette, and she has real brown hair in a double braid held in by a black net. High black shoes hide behind the pleated black silk underskirt. Her simple features—stitched lips, nose, and eyebrows, and black beaded eyes—may at first glance disappoint those who seek a pretty face. But look again. Nellie is an *original*. Now only ninety-three, she may yet, in the full ripeness of her years, astonish historians and poets, as did the "Countess of Desmond, whose death, at the age of one hundred and forty years, seems to have been less the result of age, or even of the full moon, than the result of climbing an apple tree—a strange occupation for a lady of her rank and years—and falling from this, amidst a shower of glistening apples." *Newark Museum, N.J.*

Dame Edith Sitwell, ENGLISH ECCENTRICS. Newark, N.J.: Vanguard Press, 1957, p. 42.

81.   Dame Comfort and Family, better known as The Old Woman Who
Lived in a Shoe, was made by Mrs. Mary Luyster in New England
about 1858. The shoe is 10¾ inches long and 5⅜ inches high, of black
satin with appliquéd velvet leaf, and has a wooden heel painted red. It
accommodates exactly eighteen china-head dolls, including baby in a tub.
Some have wooden bodies. The china-heads are quite rare because of
their diminutive sizes. One is reading a miniature book, written in French
script and bound in red leather. Mrs. Luyster composed a poem to accompany her handiwork.

This is little Dame Comfort presented to you.
Another old woman who lives in her shoe,
But she never gives broth without any bread,
Or whips her poor children and sends them to bed.
But she teaches them how to be happy and good,
Pay respect to their elders and never be rude;
Be kindly affectionate one to another,
And never to tease little sister or brother;
And be ready at all times to set self aside
And check the first symptoms of passion and pride.

Twenty additional rhyming lines follow. *Essex Institute, Salem, Mass.*

82. This German china doll's head from about the 1850s brings to mind the La Fontaine fable of "The Haughty Lass" who spurns her eligible suitors with logical reasons for avoiding marriage.

Wed me to wooden wits without intelligence!
Aspiring to my hand! Really! What absurdity!
Taking men as a class, a dead loss!

. . . . .

. . . I'm not here to be bought
Like girls who can't wed anyone.
Thank God I am not distraught—
Worried sick lest I be an old maid.

Fables are, with good reason, the mirror of man's (and woman's) unchanging patterns of behavior. They can be devastating in their icy reflections, admitting of no subterfuge or deceit. Does their truth make us free? I wonder . . . and I doubt that our fabled beauty will see anything in her glass until it is too late.

We can change the fashion
Of a house; but not features ravaged
by age—
Marred by pride and futile rage.*

All that she will get for her pains is to be "an uncouth fellow's wife." Can't someone shake sense into her pretty china head? *Margaret Woodbury Strong Museum of Fascination, Pittsford, N.Y.*
*THE FABLES OF LA FONTAINE, *translated by Marianne Moore. New York: Viking, 1954, pp. 148–49.*

83. It is a hot summer afternoon and they are irritated by the photographer's scurrying back and forth, his fussing with them and his heavy camera. Besides, no young lady enjoys being part of an anonymous graduating class. It is an awkward age. They are all arms and legs (wood) and their stuffed (kid) bodies are beginning to droop with fatigue. Years later they will scarcely believe that one could look so old-fashioned. The children will gasp in disbelief when Mother points to her picture (she is the fourth from the right in the last row). "Is *that you*, Ma?" And Ma, recalling younger faces and old friends, will automatically run her fingers through her hair: "I was considered a very pretty girl in *those* days." They are German papier-mâché dolls of about 1845–60, 14 to 21 inches high. *Margaret Woodbury Strong Museum of Fascination, Pittsford, N.Y.*

84. The success of the remarkable Fräulein Marga-
rete Steiff continues into the present. Her engaging
stuffed animals are recognizable to every toy-shop visitor by the well-known Steiff trademark of *Knopf im
Ohr* (button in the ear). This nostalgic scene of a tran-
quil schoolroom, about 1905–11, is a happy return to
nonbelligerent, nondropout childhood. The behavior of
the pupils is exemplary. It was not accidental. Mr.
Landshoff, the photographer, and his wife, Ursula,
author and illustrator of children's books, arranged the
dolls, as well as such details as the hats on the white
wall. Curiously, it is the hats which sum up for me
the reality of their German childhood. These Steiff
dolls are designed with the utmost simplicity—they
are anything but vapid or cute—and I believe in them
because I have seen every one in school. In short,
they are completely successful dolls. Their sizes
range from 10½ inches for the pupils to 17½ inches
for the teacher, whose name could only be Ichabod.
*Margaret Woodbury Strong Museum of Fascination,
Pittsford, N.Y.*

85. He appears to be utterly absorbed in his medita-
tive whistling, his eyes raised heavenward. I believe
he is a Down East Abolitionist of about the 1860s and
running through his wooden head, over and over again,
is the line "He is trampling out the vintage where the
grapes of wrath are stored." Having just consulted
his watch (he is acutely conscious of the passing of
time), he is waiting impatiently for the meeting to begin, when he will introduce the speaker for the evening. I daresay some child, provoked by his somber
mien, lightly penciled the cat's whiskers around his
puckered lips. He is completely wooden except for
cloth joints. His dowdy frock coat, formerly so elegant, is just a little too tight for comfort. He stands
20 inches high. *Collection Mary Merritt, Douglassville,
Pa.*

86. "Who are these hapless ones to whom evening brings no solace, to whom, like the owls, the approach of night is the signal for a witches'-sabbath?"* They loom up like skeletal figures of an early nineteenth-century Giacometti. Clothed in shapeless Directoire style, they have seen much of life. Eyes, mouth, and firmly painted eyebrows express their amused detachment. If their dresses are no longer trim, the bows on their breasts carelessly askew, what does it really matter? Only the end of summer is cause for concern. Winters are heedlessly cruel: bare rooms and thin bones, and no fire under the slanting roofs and smoke-less chimneys. At dusk, these walkers in an indifferent city pass and pass again. The night darkens and the gas lamps paint green shadows beneath their eyes.

The costumes are fashioned of orange paper and black gauze. Heads and bodies are wooden, painted green, with seal-like flippers for arms. They are French, 12 and 12¾ inches high. *Essex Institute, Salem, Mass.*

*Charles Baudelaire, PARIS SPLEEN. *New York: New Directions, 1970, p. 44.*

87. This European peg wooden family probably dates from the late nineteenth century. I have always been attracted to the homely simplicity of these woodens, which have been called Dutch dolls, Gretchens, Penny Woodens, Plain Bettys, and Woodentops. Someone was careless in painting the eyes *beneath* the nose of our smallest doll, but since penny woodens were turned out in the millions, an occasional Picassoid variation may be forgiven. In 1875, a reporter visiting Grödner Tal noted the "billions of wooden dolls, flung down helter-skelter, paid for at five farthings the dozen," and about a dozen years ago I purchased some twelve thousand of them (for resale, of course) from Mrs. Margaret Fawdry of Pollock's Toy Museum in London. She had brought them (how many?) from the Dolomites, where they had been stored in a barn. They continue to be available in toy shops, though the supply should be close to extinction. My daughter's collection contains a group of several half- and one-inch woodens. This family ranges in size from 8½ to 12½ inches. *New-York Historical Society.*

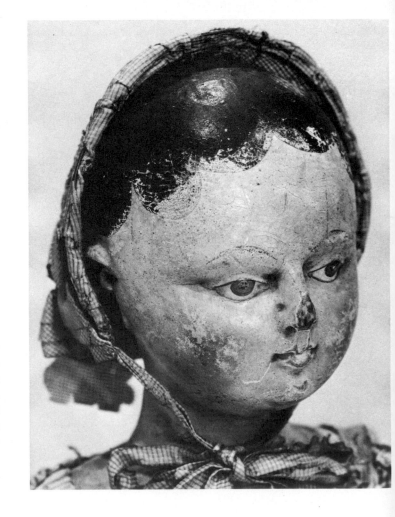

88. A tall wooden doll, 24 inches high, from late eighteenth-century France, she was a manikin sent to America wearing the fashionable dress of the period. It is said that she was the favorite of a Quaker child some 150 years ago. Now she wears a brown-and-white flowered dress and a checked bonnet. Her eyes are blue, her cheeks are flushed, and she has painted brown hair. It is not said how she suffered her chipped nose. Despite this sign of excessive love, she retains a freshness of spirit not often seen in one so old. *Atwater Kent Museum, Philadelphia, Pa.*

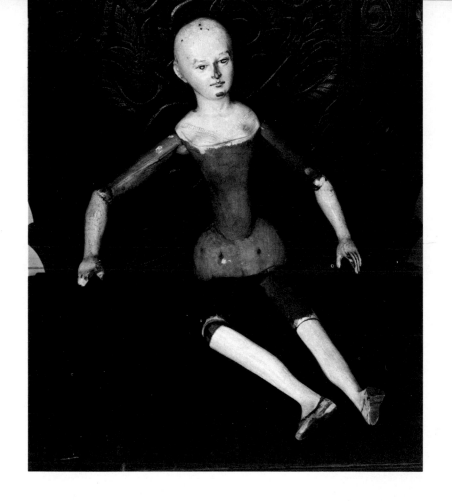

89. It is said that Nathaniel Arden brought this jointed wooden doll from Europe sometime before 1797. Those superlative doll collectors Ruth E. and R. C. Mathes suggest that it is from a French or Italian crèche of the seventeenth or eighteenth century. An eighteenth-century bodice is indicated; there are nail marks on the head where a wig had been stretched; but ball-and-socket joints in the arms and legs suggest the earlier century. Though I do not disagree with Mr. and Mrs. Mathes, I see no expression in the young woman of what I look upon as religiosity. No matter. She has been taken by surprise. Clothing would have made all the difference. Height 24 inches. *Essex Institute, Salem, Mass.*

90. In a collection that boasts numerous fine old dolls, this one is said to be the rarest and is perhaps the loveliest. One of many in a museum case, she has here been transformed by her new environment. Suddenly she becomes part of her time and place—about 1820–40 in the United States. Her rubber head has deep black eyes and hair painted black over long, flowing molded curls. Her body and legs are of stuffed cotton. She wears a purple silk print dress with sleeves puffed to below the elbow, a slip with tatting, knee-length pantalettes, black cotton stockings, and black leather slippers. She is 26¾ inches high. *Essex Institute, Salem, Mass.*

91.   All we know about our 16-inch knitted black doll (standing) is that she was made by Mrs. Sarah Kimball, who was born on July 20, 1814, was the widow, at seventy-eight, of Elias Kimball, and died on February 27, 1895. What the photograph does not reveal is the trimness of the doll's waist, the fashionable figure of a proud woman, sturdy, shaped legs and upright bearing of shoulders—in all, an independent young person. I do not doubt that this is a portrait. Was she a friend of Mrs. Kimball's? The matching pattern of stockings, skirt, sweater, and hatband is uniquely right. Of all the dolls we have seen, she is the only one I would recommend for reproduction, and I offer myself as the first buyer.

The seated rag doll, also black, is from Barbados, about 1913. She balances a tray holding a sack and a bundle of wood. Her bead eyes are outlined in white thread and red thread draws a line for her mouth. Her nose and chin have been shaped and her ears sewn on. She wears neither shoes nor socks. Both dolls *Essex Institute, Salem, Mass.*

92.   William Steig is one of a dwindling group of cartoonists whose drawings I have long admired. It was with much delight that we discovered a creation of his, the doll named Poor, Pitiful Pearl. But I could not find out anything about Pearl until it occurred to me to write the man who knew her better than anyone else.

"Pearl was originally produced by Glad Toy Co. in the middle fifties and until about 1960. It was revived by Horsman Dolls in the middle sixties. It is no longer being made. It was an idea that I had in my drawer a long time before I got around to making a model. Pearl was an *orphan* who was to be *adopted* by the kid who got her. I wanted her to be sold with real dirt on her face and unkempt hair so she could be washed and combed before being dressed in the party dress she came with. (I assume you know that she was sold with a party dress and that advertisements showed 'before' and 'after' pictures.) But the manufacturer felt one couldn't sell a dirty doll. Pearl is in the style of 'Small Fry,' a series of children I used to do for *The New Yorker*." She stands 16 inches high. *Collection Margaret D. Patterson, Sand Lake, N.Y.*

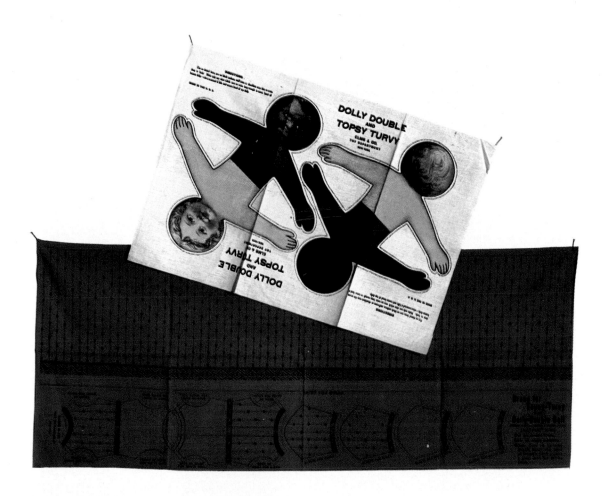

93. Two dolls in one, Dolly Double and Topsy Turvy are cutout rag dolls with printed cotton material for the making of their dresses. They are probably from the nineteenth century, and are 12 inches high. Their happy, open-armed greeting would in time become an endearing memory to their one-time owners. Dating from a time when the Negro was often caricatured, this is a refreshing portrait, honestly observed. Whoever the artist, he seems to have had some training in sculpture; both heads are almost three-dimensional, front and back. The curling hair of the white child is reminiscent of the modeling of a Renaissance master. *Collection Margaret Whitton, Bridgewater, Conn.*

94. This rag doll is from the United States, about 1800–25, and is 29 inches high. There is no concealing the toil of years, the flabby muscles, the absence of all vanity. But her eyes are still clear. Her face, like her lower arms and hands, has been painted in oil colors. Amateurs at sewing did their best to keep her intact. In any collection of American folk art she would have an honored place. *Collection Leo and Dorothy Rabkin, New York City.*

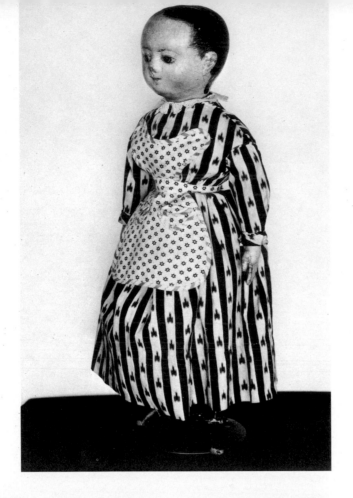

95–96. She is one of the most appealing of American dolls. Patented in 1873 by Miss Izannah F. Walker of Central Falls, Rhode Island, this humble rag doll with oil-painted face is found in numerous collections. She is as beautiful to me now as when I saw her for the first time in Miss Walker's cabinet. How could one not fall deeply in love with her? She is a *presence*, a serene, understanding confidante. There is no end to the mysteries of her face as she changes with the brightness or fading of the light. She is 18½ inches high. *Collection Frances Walker.*

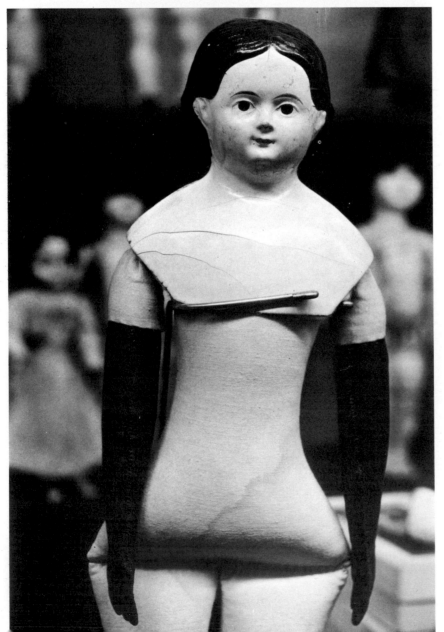

97. "My story is ended, and I, Victoria-Bess, have only one thing more to add, which is briefly this—to beg of you, little children, who read my story, never to throw us dolls away into the dust-bin; but when ceasing to please you and to minister to your happiness (having grown faded and ugly, either from time or accident), you care no longer to keep us—send us where dear Miss Binney took *me* this Christmastide, to an Hospital for Sick Children, where in spite of broken noses, and cracked heads, and faded garments, we shall be received and warmly welcomed, and where, perchance, we may find a kind little mistress, like Moggy, to throw her arm around us and comfort us in our old age.''*

She has a papier-mâché head with painted eyes, a body of stuffed muslin, and arms of kid. She was made in the United States about 1870 and her height is 18 inches. *New York Doll Hospital.*

Brenda [Mrs. Castle Smith], "Victoria-Bess: The Ups and Downs of a Doll's Life," in VICTORIAN DOLL STORIES. *New York: Schocken, 1969.*

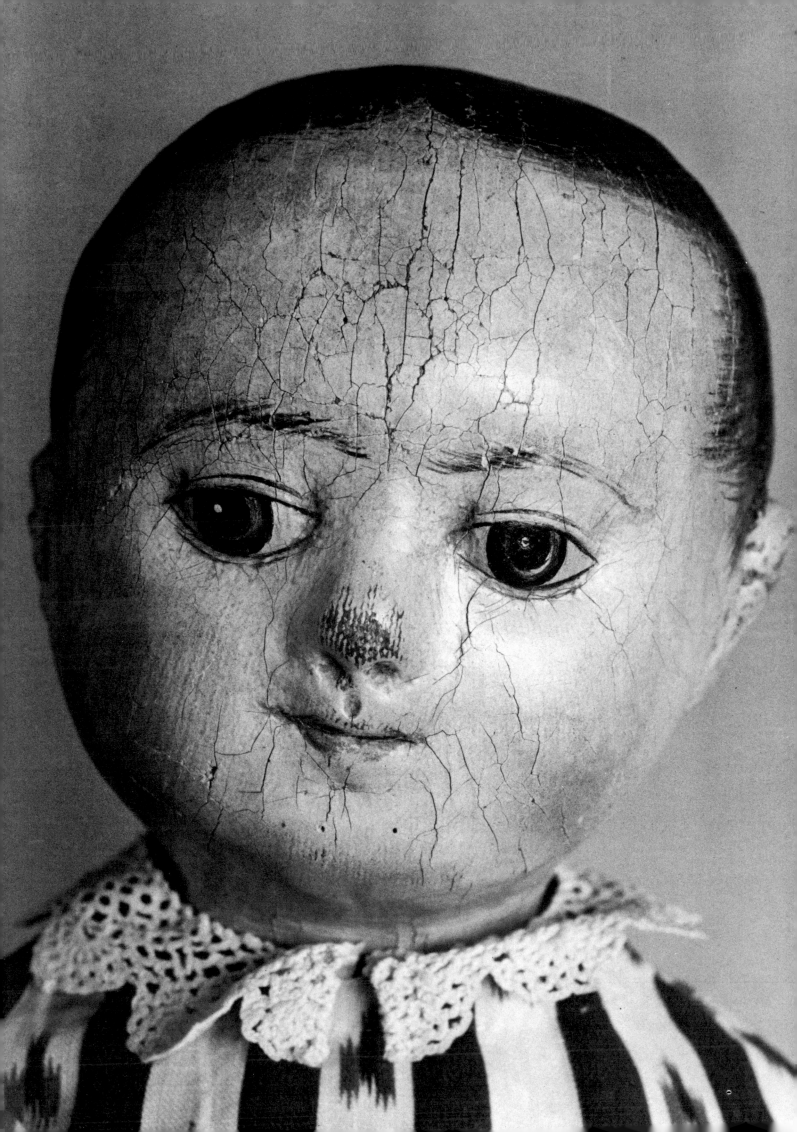

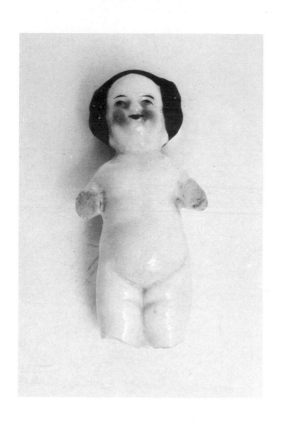

98. Reminiscent of the Paleolithic limestone idol known as the *Venus of Willendorf*, although in no way similar, she has black hair, blue eyes, pink cheeks, and very red lips. A goddess of love? An earth goddess of spring? Alas, no. She is a fragment of a Frozen Charlotte doll, just 2¾ inches high. She is German, probably late nineteenth century. Manufactured in the tens of millions and sold for pennies, she is the essence of Middle European taste, of what our elders thought every woman (and child) should be—pleasingly plump. *Collection Leo and Dorothy Rabkin, New York City.*

99.. Can one naked doll be more naked than another? These china bathing babies, popularly called Frozen Charlottes—or in this case Frozen Charlies—are eagerly waiting to enter the gentlemen's Turkish bath. Their healthy, pink-tinted bodies and heads are fresh from a vigorous workout in the gymnasium. I find them droll—they look like stolid citizens, their administrative futures already assured. They are German, about 1850–1914, and are from 8 to 16 inches high. *Margaret Woodbury Strong Museum of Fascination, Pittsford, N.Y.*

100. From Germany, the United States, and Mexico come these dolls and dolls'
heads, all of them bisque except the porcelain baby in the tub, ranging in size from
1 to 4 inches. Some are late nineteenth century, some early twentieth. Small and vulnerable, each doll of this motley collection is transformed, upon exploration of its shape
and texture, into an individual once snugly concealed in the small hand of a child—safe
from a careless foot, an envious playmate, a spiteful sister. How difficult it is not to
open one's fingers and reveal the secret! *Collection Leo and Dorothy Rabkin, New York
City.*

101. What harrowing experience has made the doll on the left almost bald? An English Montanari type, her head and limbs are made of molded hollow wax. These are protected by metal grommets where they are sewn onto the stuffed muslin body. The pale blue dress is not original. Somewhere along the way she was given a gold locket and chain. It is her only possession.

Someone probably threw the center doll into the fire. Her dress was burned, and only her undergarments were preserved. Her head is wax over composition, her arms wax, and her legs composition with painted boots. Her left arm seems to have been broken. She is English, about 1870.

Thought to have been made in England in the late nineteenth century, the doll at right wears her original dress over wax legs and a cloth body. She has not been too badly neglected, but her sorrow is profound. Like the others, she measures 24 inches. *Collection Frances Walker.*

102. They are French bisque, except for the small doll in the lower right corner who pushed herself forward at the last moment: she is German bisque; heights range from 14 to 26 inches. (1) "F.G.," made by F. Gaultier, about 1885. (2) and (3) Tête Jumeau, about 1885. (4) Steiner, about 1880. (5) Paris Bébé, about 1890. (6) Jumeau, about 1880. (7) the little German, about 1880–85. *Collection Grace Dyar, Hartford, Conn.*

104. These are good examples from the contemporary school which believes that "less is more." They are among the most durable dolls. The two roped to each other like mountain climbers in the Alps, where they were made, are 5 inches high and fit snugly into the hand. The colored plastic acrobats, called Whimsicals, are 4 inches high; are they perhaps symbolic of the faceless society of the future? When I was younger, I was impressed and dismayed by *R.U.R.*, the play by Karel Capek, whose Rossum's Universal Robots I thought a farfetched and ridiculous idea. But there are now more things in heaven and earth than were then dreamt of in my philosophy. *Creative Playthings.*

103. Of course they have always been called ninepins, but for me, as a young child, my ninepins were my dolls, as was Teddy Bear and almost any toy shaped like a human being or an animal. These German military ninepins of the late nineteenth century have muttonchop whiskers that are once again to be seen on the men we meet every day. They are an erect 12¼ inches high, including their stands. I must say that they look like a kindly group of warriors. *Wenham Historical Association, Wenham, Mass.*

105.   Who among us has never loved a Kewpie? The
continue to be irresistible. Although they verge on ca
icature, the charm of Rose O'Neill's concept keep
them from going over the edge, and the worst I coul
say about Kewpie is that she is cute. But utterly be
guiling. Even as a small child, I much admired Ros
O'Neill's illustrations and thought that each faci
drawing was a masterpiece to be copied in crayon
The worldwide success story of Kewpie has been tol
many times, best of all in a copiously illustrated biog
raphy by Mrs. Rowena Godding Ruggles.* The com
mercial success of Kewpies may remain unsurpasse
made, as they have been, in every material and repr
duced in an endless succession of souvenirs; one ca
not estimate the tens of millions of dolla
garnered by Kewpie in over half a century. Our sma
collection does not begin to illuminate the comple
Kewpie phenomenon. This group measures from 1
to 9 inches. *Margaret Woodbury Strong Museum
Fascination, Pittsford, N.Y.*

*THE ONE ROSE. *Oakland, Calif.: Rowena Goddin
Ruggles, 1964.*

106.   She announces her presence by tapping rhythmi-
cally on the bell. One can respond in either of two
ways: by hiding behind the window blinds or, if attracted to her nose-in-the-air beauty, by welcoming her
with praise for her tricycling skill. Yes, she has been
spoiled by indulgent parents, but her delight is conta-
gious, and I would be quick to climb up behind with
my arms around her waist; the clockwork mechanism
would do the cycling for both of us. She is a composition doll made in the United States in about 1860, and
is 8½ inches high. She is prettily dressed in a black
velvet jacket, pink taffeta skirt, and blue satin pillbox
hat with a pink rose. *New-York Historical Society.*

PLATES 107—145

107. This French mechanical swimming doll was, we believe, made by a man named Martin and exhibited in 1879 at the Exposition Universelle in Paris, where the simultaneous movements of her arms and legs attracted much favorable attention. She has a bisque head, wooden body, and metal hands. Her expertise permits her to swim without wetting her hair—an important accomplishment for any female swimmer. From toes to fingertips she is 18½ inches. *Margaret Woodbury Strong Museum of Fascination, Pittsford, N.Y.*

108. When Ives, Blakeslee & Williams of Bridgeport, Connecticut, manufactured this pull toy, about 1870 or so, it was advertised in their catalogue as: "No 71 Iron Shoe. An assortment of children. Size 6½ by 9 inches. Price per doz . . . . . .$12.00. The Shoe is Mounted on Wheels and is to be drawn along by a string. The Dolls can be removed and replaced." The shoe sported a large bow and the children numbered seven in the engraving, along with their mother, who wore a frilled cotton bonnet. But the children have grown up and only one child remains to enjoy the ride. The dolls, mother and daughter, have metal mask faces. *Collection Margaret Whitton, Bridgewater, Conn.*

109. This panoramic scene of 5½-inch-high bisque bathing beauties from Germany (probably early 1920s) in peek-a-boo bathing suits utterly captivates me. If this is *Kitsch*, then I make the most of it. In surveying the thousands of dolls in the Strong collection, I knew at once that these were meant for me. A song from Gilbert and Sullivan's *Princess Ida* could not be suppressed, and I found myself singing:

Would you know the kind of maid
    Sets my heart a-flame-a?
Eyes must be downcast and staid,
    Cheeks must flush for shame-a!
She may neither dance nor sing,
    But, demure in everything,
Hang her head in modest way,
With pouting lips that seem to say,
''Oh, kiss me, kiss me, kiss me, kiss me,
    Though I die of shame-a!''
Please you, that's the kind of maid
    Sets my heart a-flame-a!

Margaret Woodbury Strong Museum of Fascination,
Pittsford, N.Y.

110. Our stockinette boy doll wears a white blouse, black satin cap and suit, white stockings, and black shoes. He has been sitting in his chair in the corner waiting for someone to pick him up. Many dolls do not really care; some complain; others do not wish to be disturbed. But he was made to be held—this is his reason for being—and so he continues to look expectantly at each passing visitor. He is from the United States, about 1896, and is 27 inches high. *New-York Historical Society*.

111. The Bye-Lo Baby doll was created by the American sculptress Grace Storey Putnam, whose search for an ideal baby led her through all the hospitals in Los Angeles. The 1922 copyright describes the photographed wax head as "life-sized, modeled from a baby three days old, eyes slightly narrowed, mouth closed, fat rolls at back of neck." Before the head was manufactured in bisque, the eyes were opened and some of the rolls of fat were removed. One of the most natural-looking dolls, the Bye-Lo Baby may be too real for some collectors, doll lovers, and educators. This is not an abstraction of a baby; it is a portrait whose realistically shaped head reaffirms my own observations and those of Mrs. Putnam. Over the years, her Million Dollar Baby has been produced in various mediums—celluloid, bisque, composition, rubber—as well as in a limited lifesize edition in wax. Our collection ranges in size from 4 to 20 inches. *Margaret Woodbury Strong Museum of Fascination, Pittsford, N.Y.*

112. As with so many dolls, his history is unknown. Many of these anonymous orphan children still bear signs of the love shown them by their companion-owners, who dressed the dolls as best they could with whatever material they found or could beg from their elders. His collar and cuffs may have been scraps from a discarded curtain; washed and ironed, the pieces were folded and sewn in place to transform the plain velvet into a party suit. His shapeless gray shoes and gray stockings are crude but clean. His papier-mâché face has been scrubbed until his light blue eyes have all but lost their color. He is from the United States, about the nineteenth century; his height is 15½ inches. *New-York Historical Society*.

113. These bisque dolls, boy and girl, are dressed in Pennsylvania Dutch style. She wears a faded and worn lavender silk dress, black cape and bonnet, and high black boots. Her blond hair is soft and real. Her eyes are painted light blue. She has not used her boots, size 3; neither has her companion, who has smaller feet, shoe size 2½. He is dressed in black, all wool from hat to cape to long coat, trousers, and stockings. His hair and eyes are painted brown. They are not really as unhappy as they look; they are just filled beyond their capacity with Spätzle, Schnitzbrot, and Lebkuchen. It will take several hours to recover from their celebration of Second Christmas. She stands (when she can) 16¾ inches, and he 17¾ inches high. They probably date from the late nineteenth century. *Atwater Kent Museum, Philadelphia, Pa.*

114. They have wandered into Vollard's gallery on the Rue Lafitte because Vollard is known to have the latest thing in painting. But what is exhibited on the walls is really too much. It is an assault on their intelligence.

In her vexation, the young lady on the left has dropped her hat. She is the shortest (24 inches high) of the three bisque Jumeaus, and dates from about 1875. Her close friend, who dates about 1875–80, is 27 inches high. Our last defender of the Academy is 26 inches high and dates about 1890–95. She is the only one with graceful bisque hands. It's been a trying day and she has lost one of her kid gloves. *Margaret Woodbury Strong Museum of Fascination, Pittsford, N.Y.*

115. This bisque doll, made in Paris by A. Marque early in our century, has a composition body, bisque arms and legs, and real blond hair. She is dressed in what appears to be a peasant costume, French or Alsatian. One of her distinguishing characteristics is the series of little lines painted on her eyelids. She seems to come to sculptural points at her nose, lips, and chin. She is one of those children whose features early assume the mask of adulthood. Her height is 22 inches. *Margaret Woodbury Strong Museum of Fascination, Pittsford, N.Y.*

116. My urge is to call them Tom, Dick, and Harry, after the young heroes whose courage, hard work, and luck (mostly luck) were so enthusiastically documented by Horatio Alger, Jr., beginning in 1865 with *Tom Thatcher's Fortune*. All have wax heads; the bodies contain a talking mechanism, now silent. No doubt they spoke, as Alger characters did, in capital letters. Tom is 15 inches, Dick is 12¼ inches, and Harry is 14 inches high. All three have painted blue wooden shoes. They date from about 1880 and were made in the United States. *New-York Historical Society.*

117. Time has been cruel to her, but it has not erased her pale, faint smile. Long ago she was a black doll. According to information supplied by the Essex Institute, the knowledgeable Ruth E. and R. C. Mathes believe she was an "early Queen Anne. Only the torso remains; arms and legs have been replaced by rag ones, the torso painted brown and a wig of tiny black curls added. Her face is badly battered but the glass eyes (one broken) indicate her early origin. She was probably re-dressed toward 1840–1860." Truly nobody knows the troubles she's seen. *Essex Institute, Salem, Mass.*

118. Bright-eyed Hope Richardson, born about 1857, is bubbling with suppressed gaiety. She has a perfectly round wax head with real curls, not embedded, and still wears her original peach-colored silk dress. Whenever I look at her, I too must smile. A smug but congenial companion. She is 21 inches high, of unknown provenance. *Essex Institute, Salem, Mass.*

119. Even in the most nondescript clothing, bisque Jumeau Bébés have a seductive charm, like the early Renoir paintings of children, pretty but not saccharine. The Bébés in the first two rows are 9¼ to 12 inches high, in the top row 15½ to 17 inches high. Nineteenth century. *Margaret Woodbury Strong Museum of Fascination, Pittsford, N.Y.*

120. Of all the dolls here reviewed, she is the happiest. It is presumed that she is French, made in Paris during the 1890s for the colonies. Her head is bisque, her glass eyes are brown, her body is composition, and she stands 16 inches high. She is wearing four skirts, each of a different gingham fabric; her bodice is eyelet lace. Around her neck is a string of leather containers which may once have held a secret (love?) potion. *Margaret Woodbury Strong Museum of Fascination, Pittsford, N.Y.*

121.   She has walked (because she is a key-wind walking doll) into the General Store for a package of dates. While the little gentleman—a German dollhouse doll of her vintage, about 1890, with bisque head and legs—counts her change, she is wondering if she should purchase additional party favors. Probably from Nuremberg, she is 12 inches high, with bisque head, blond wig, glass eyes, jointed composition arms, and body and legs of metal. The penny woodens are from Austria, Germany, France, and England and are early nineteenth century. *Wenham Historical Association, Wenham, Mass.*

122. "In 1795, Susanna Holyoke went to a ball at the Assembly House on Federal Street, and her maid accompanied her. Returning home, the maid dressed this doll in exact imitation of one of the elegantly dressed ladies she saw at the ball." Some of our stories are apocryphal, but I repeat them because everyone loves a story, true or not. This English wooden Queen Anne type, 11 inches high, with kid arms and legs, wears her original and now threadbare lace-trimmed clothes of pink silk. The saucy hat atop her dark hair is white tulle with pink roses and green leaves. She is a period piece, sharply observed and recorded for our delight. Too early to be called Dickensian, she is a unique contribution to the doll world. *Wenham Historical Association, Wenham, Mass.*

123. I have always regarded this wooden doll as one of the great American "primitive" carvings. My feeling was strengthened when I learned that she had been in the collection of the sculptor Elie Nadelman, who, along with his wife, was among the early "discoverers" of American folk art. If we must have monuments, I can see her as a happy monument to the pioneer woman. She is only 9½ inches high, but, like all great sculpture, she could just as well tower to 9½ feet. If her eighteenth-century birthdate is correct, how wonderful for us that she has survived so well in her painted dress, with its red and black polka dots. She may be seen in the splendid collection of toys, dolls, and American folk art at the *New-York Historical Society.*

125. Was this leather doll made by a shoemaker for his daughter? This suggests itself because of the skill with which the leather is shaped, the use of metal eyelets, and the shoelace tying in the cotton stuffing. Was she the result of his idle afternoons before Christmas? Her small features are tooled, her nose and chin slightly pinched, her hair painted black. I am unhappy about the stitching that bisects her face. Wouldn't you have thought that an old-time shoemaker would have been particularly careful to conceal the stitches at the side of her head? But that is a technical criticism and in no way mitigates the love he felt for his daughter and her doll. It is assumed that she was made in the United States during the nineteenth century; her height is 12½ inches. *Margaret Woodbury Strong Museum of Fascination, Pittsford, N.Y.*

124. This wooden doll from Europe, about 1788–1800, is 18 inches high and has ball-and-socket joints; her hair and her features are painted. She is dressed as a Quaker—according to legend, in France. Indeed, she is threadbare, and we would like to believe that a Frenchwoman made for a Philadelphian her impression of a beautiful young Quaker. Her face, which has been covered with lacquer, has turned a not unpleasant yellow, but her cheeks are still pink. No doubt it is the air from the Schuylkill River. *Atwater Kent Museum, Philadelphia, Pa.*

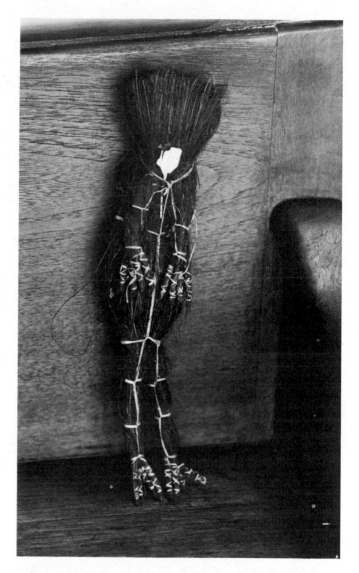

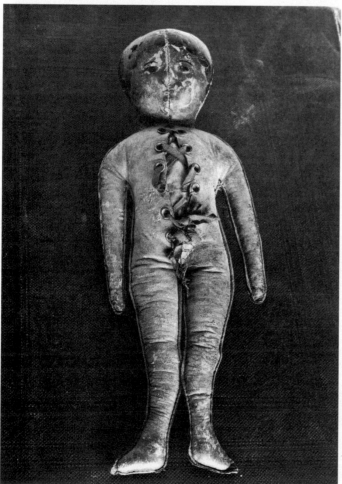

126. This faceless, most primitive of dolls is crudely made of dark brown fibers folded and bound to form a body, head, arms, legs, feet with four toes, and hands with four fingers. Max von Boehn illustrates a similar "magic doll" from the Celebes and writes that "male figures are worked out of fibre bound round with strips of bast; as soon as the priest has charmed the disease into them these substitutes for the patients are removed . . . and cast, along with their evil spirits, into the sea."* From the Celebes, Indonesia, about 1917–20, he is 11¾ inches high. *Peabody Museum, Salem, Mass.*

*DOLLS AND PUPPETS, *translated by Josephine Nicoll. Boston: Charles J. Branford, rev. ed. 1956, p. 62.*

127.   For those who are skeptical about using German military ninepins for dolls, that stalwart group is here translated into a series of cutout rag dolls—Soldier Boys, patented by the Arnold Print Works in 1892. Does it matter whether they are made of wood, paper, or stuffed cotton? Not to me. Our Soldier Boys stand upright at 8 inches. *Collection Margaret Whitton, Bridgewater, Conn.*

129. In numbers and in its generosity of spirit, the Strong collection of dolls resembles the charitable Foundling Hospital of London (founded 1739), where "a basket was hung at the gate of the hospital for the reception of infants [read "dolls"] and notice of each arrival was given by the clanging of a great iron bell. So great, indeed, was the demand for admission that between the years 1756 and 1760, 14,900 children were admitted. The hospital was unable to accommodate the foundlings presented to it so that the mothers [read "dealers"] who brought them were all obliged to wait outside the gate while they balloted with balls out of a bag to see which children would be admitted or thrown back on the world."*

Mrs. Strong followed in the tradition of the private collectors of the past, whose insatiable acquisition of art led to the use of cabinets for curiosities and finally to the establishment of museums. The dolls pictured here are bisques, chinas, and parians (porcelains) from France, Germany, and Denmark, about 1850–1910. *Margaret Woodbury Strong Museum of Fascination, Pittsford, N.Y.*

*Francis Henry Taylor, THE TASTE OF ANGELS. Boston: Little, Brown, 1948, p. 470.

128. We stopped for breakfast along the New Jersey Turnpike. Later, browsing among the souvenirs, we found these United States Spacemen— "Unbreakable Action Figures, Realistically Detailed, Not Less than 58 Figures," manufactured by Multiple Toymakers of New York. In a decade or less, these dolls will find their way into junk shops across America. This continuing preoccupation with nostalgia embraces almost everything made by man. It is no longer who you are or what you are that matters: it is what you collect. Nothing is too outrageous for the shopkeepers to call "cultural antiques" or—I hope with tongue in cheek— "new antiques."

130. At first glance I called her Ophelia, and Ophelia she remains. There is a madness in her eyes and smile: "She is importunate, indeed distract." Her high, thin voice can still be heard: "Come, my coach! Good night, ladies, good night. Sweet ladies, good night, good night." She wears a coronet of flowers on an ash-blond wig fashioned of human hair, which is human-head size but pressed to fit her wax-over-papier-mâché head. She is English, about 1830, and is 29½ inches high. The arms and hands are kidskin. She wears an iridescent green and red silk-taffeta dress trimmed with white ruching, white pantalettes edged with crochet work, white stockings, and black dancing pumps. *Collection Mary Merritt, Douglassville, Pa.*

132. This demure young wax-over-papier-mâché doll from England or France, about 1830–40, with cloth body and arms, is wearing a pink net Empire dress. She has two petticoats and underclothing of cambric, knitted stockings, and black velvet slippers. A wire beneath her dress opens and closes her heavy-lidded eyes. Her height is 15 inches. When I went back to Newark to check on her background, I found her asleep in her cardboard box, her eyes tightly closed. We did not disturb her. *Newark Museum, N.J.*

131. I am captivated by their assurance, their lack of modesty, their belief that "all is for the best in the best of possible worlds." One would devoutly wish to agree with them, but we have been born too late.

From left to right:

(1) French, about 1870, she has a bisque head and ball-and-socket-jointed wooden body and arms. Her height is 17 inches.

(2) Our next bisque beauty has attained a certain amount of fame. In 1864 she was exhibited at the New York Sanitary Fair and was named Miss Flora McFlimsy of Madison Square after the poem "Nothing to Wear," written in 1857 by William A. Butler. Her height is 17 inches.

(3) A French or German doll of about 1870, she is 16 inches high, her head bisque, her body leather.

(4) French, about 1870, 16½ inches tall, she is a bisque doll who has suffered the loss of both hands. But she does have a change of dress (standing beside her), which has seen better days. *New-York Historical Society.*

133. Just as it did for Miss Havisham in *Great Expectations*, time halted for this doll many years ago, and what she chooses to remember of her glorious chapeau (she stopped looking in mirrors long ago) still exists for her, if not for the rest of us, who may smile at the pretensions of her ravaged silk hat. Someone has re-dressed her in the Empire style, in figured lawn cotton. She is wooden, the gesso flaking in spots, her blue glass eyes inlaid and slightly protuberant. Her eyes and eyelashes are rimmed with tiny painted dots. Her body is square-bottomed and her arms are of mottled white leather. She is English, probably from the nineteenth century. Height 15 inches. *Chester County Historical Society, West Chester, Pa.*

134. The French Jumeaus are among the aristocrats of the doll world. Certainly their beauty of face and costume is almost always strikingly evident. Here is an exception. What could have prompted this shorn-lamb's-wool wig, the dowdy, fussy moire dress, black stockings and shoes? Somewhere along her journey, exchanging owners, she was put together by someone who did not see the fair Jumeau below the wig. She reminds me of the consternation with which I greeted my mother's newly bobbed hair in the 1920s. Our Jumeau has brown glass eyes and wears earrings in her pierced ears. Probably made in the late nineteenth century, she is 19½ inches high. *Margaret Woodbury Strong Museum of Fascination, Pittsford, N.Y.*

135. One is astonished that she has survived, this English breadcrumb doll who has been dated, perhaps optimistically, about 1820. Her head, which measures exactly 2¼ inches, should long ago have been a number of tasty mouthfuls for enterprising rodents, perhaps Beatrix Potter's two bad mice, Tom Thumb and his spouse Hunca Munca. Our laughing doll lady wears a respectable bonnet as well as a crocheted woolen frill cap and a rough cloak. She is 12 inches high, with kid arms and a stuffed cloth body. *Collection Mary Merritt, Douglassville, Pa.*

136. We presume they are bride and bridesmaids. But what is the meaning of the blown-glass antlered stag that the bride holds? Is it a stag at bay? Does it symbolize the captivity of her husband-to-be? It is a joyless beginning. And yet the bride is not as intimidating as the bridesmaids. She is *not* implacable. She *will* be a faithful wife and loving mother.

The attending dolls in the rear are 10 inches high; their small bosoms are decorated with sequined hearts. The bride wears organdy trimmed with silk lace and taffeta ribbon sewn with sequins. She stands two inches above the 20-inch bridesmaids. The dolls are English, about 1835, and are made of wax over papier-mâché, with kid bodies, arms, and hands. *Collection Mary Merritt, Douglassville, Pa.*

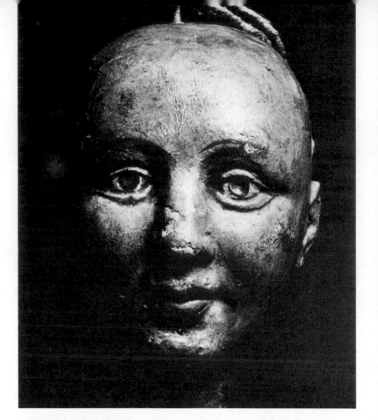

138. Twenty-five years ago there was a shop on the East Side of New York that dealt in magic and spells. In the romantic gloom, surrounded by esoteric objects understood only by diabolists who could evoke the Foul Fiend, our photographer was struck by one pure, radiant object. It was this Sicilian puppet head, probably nineteenth century. Puppet heads continue to be carved in Sicily, but I have never seen another so unforgettable.

137. This doll's beautiful face illuminated the darkness of the dimly lighted basement storage room where we found him. His felt hat suggests that he was made late in the nineteenth century in the United States. He was, it is believed, a hand puppet. His wooden head measures 4½ inches in height. *New-York Historical Society.*

139. This 3½-inch wax doll from Haiti wears a checked dress. Her age is unknown, but she is probably of this century. One is prone to associate wax dolls from Haiti with voodoo. We do not know. Her downcast eyes seem to be brooding on things beyond experience. If there is a mystery to be read in her inscrutable face, I have not read it. Sometimes I believe she was made by a blind person creating a face known only by touch. *Collection Leo and Dorothy Rabkin, New York City.*

140. A baby doll from France, about 1835–50, she is 20½ inches high and was made by Maison Munnier of Paris. She has a wax-over-papier-mâché head, lower limbs, and feet, and glass, wire-pull eyes. Her body contains a mechanism for kicking and turning. The open mouth reveals tiny upper and lower teeth. She is wearing a long white dress trimmed with lace and blue ribbons. A bracelet with blue stones circles her wrist. Her skin has turned quite saffron, but she was very much alive and kicking when I last saw her. *Newark Museum, N.J.*

141. Our brooding German papier-mâché doll, of about 1880, has molded light brown hair, painted eyes, and a stuffed muslin body with papier-mâché arms. She is 24 inches high. *New York Doll Hospital.*

143. He stands debonairly before the cardboard boxes of Newark's splendid collection of American dolls. He is dressed in bluish-green velveteen trousers and rust-colored velveteen shirt. He was exactly one hundred years old in 1970. There is every reason to believe he will celebrate another centennial in the year 2070. *Newark Museum.*

142. Our French Jumeau is proudest of her print dress, its fabric inspired by the cashmere shawl in the portrait of Madame Leblanc painted by Ingres in Florence in 1823. It was by the sheerest chance that our doll's mother saw the portrait. When the printed fabric patterned after the Kashmirian original began to be manufactured, she was the first to buy some yardage to make this dress for her daughter, who dates from about 1880–85 and is 14 inches high. *New York Doll Hospital.*

144. It has been suggested that she comes from Martinique. In which case it is feasible to assume that she was made by a native woman for her French mistress in about 1830. She stands 11¼ inches high in a cotton dress of fine quality; her head and body are made of kidskin. *Collection Mary Meritt, Douglassville, Pa.*

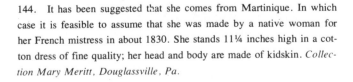

145.   These six French bisque Bébés are from the second half of the nineteenth century. On the left is a 19-inch Jumeau with composition body. The doll in front of her is 14 inches high; her head bears the initials "E.J." The Bébé in yellow is a 19-inch doll whose head is marked "R.D."—probably the doll makers Rabery and Delphieu. The other doll in the foreground, 14 inches high, was made by Steiner. The doll behind her, 20 inches high, has pewter hands; marked "P.D.," she was probably made by Petit and Dumoutier. At the extreme right, another Steiner, 19 inches high, with composition body. All the ladies have pierced ears and all predate the use of weighted eyes. *Collection Frances Walker.*

NOTES

"*The fact is that in the making of notes—of which to some minds there should be no beginning—it is difficult to find an end.*

"*Still, it must be confessed that some of the pages that follow are not only without rhyme, but with very little detectable reason. An even larger number are, in fact, confessions of ignorance. For of all the boys in a school, it is the dunce who—if only he were encouraged—could ask the most questions. He may by no means be the best at answering them for himself: but the attempt to do so, even when it is made with so little method and so much at random as it has been here, is its own reward.*"

WALTER DE LA MARE
Come Hither: A Collection of Rhymes and Poems for the Young of All Ages.

1. "This supreme quality is felt by the artist when the esthetic image is first conceived in his imagination. The mind in that mysterious instant Shelley likened beautifully to a fading coal. The instant wherein that supreme quality of beauty, the clear radiance of the esthetic image, is apprehended luminously by the mind which has been arrested by its wholeness and fascinated by its harmony is the luminous silent stasis of esthetic pleasure, a spiritual state very like to that cardiac condition which the Italian physiologist Luigi Galvani, using a phrase almost as beautiful as Shelley's, called the enchantment of the heart."

James Joyce, *A Portrait of the Artist as a Young Man.* New York: Viking Press, 1964, p. 213.

2. "Great works of art, Nietzsche once said, have an element of mystery that cannot be fully explained. It is this inexplicable air of mystery which makes such a strong impression when we view Leonardo's portrait of Ginevra de' Benci. The picture casts a spell but when we attempt to explain fully its mysterious fascination and beauty its secret eludes us."

Perry B. Cott, *Leonardo's Portrait of Ginevra de' Benci.* Washington, D.C.: National Gallery of Art, 1967.

3. "But the first necessity is that the artist should render the image; if there are no images there are no ideas, and a civilization slowly but inevitably dies."

Sir Herbert Read, "Art and Society," in *The Arts and Man.* Englewood Cliffs, N.J.: Prentice-Hall, and Paris: UNESCO, 1969, p. 37.

4. Edward Lear, "The Story of the Four Little Children Who Went Around the World," in *The Complete Nonsense Book.* New York: Dodd, Mead & Co., 1946, p. 37.

5. Whether it is Wallace Stevens' "Thirteen Ways of Looking at a Blackbird" or Hokusai's *One Hundred Views of Mt. Fuji*, the author, artist, and photographer have an insatiable curiosity to see all sides of the object; nor are they discouraged if it should take a lifetime, as it often does the man of genius. Because I am not a man of genius, I stand in awe of the Japanese artist Hokusai who at the age of seventy-five wrote: "From the age of six I had a mania for drawing the forms of things. By the time I was fifty I had published an infinity of designs; but all I produced before the age of seventy is not worth taking into account. At seventy-three I learned a little about the real structure of nature, of animals, plants, trees, birds, fishes, and insects. In consequence, when I am eighty I shall have made still more progress; at ninety I shall penetrate the mystery of things; at a hundred I shall certainly have reached a marvelous stage; and when I am a hundred and ten everything I do, be it a dot or a line, will be alive. I beg those who live as long as I to see if I do not keep my word."
Quoted by James A. Michener in *The Hokusai Sketch-Books: Selections from the "Manga."* Rutland, Vt.: Charles E. Tuttle Co., 1958, p. 20.

6. "Just as every boy had his jackknife, every little girl had her dolls. Even in the earliest settlements little Puritan mothers cherished their doll babies made of cloth or wood. In 1800 most little girls still played with and loved the same kind of homemade dolls, wooden dolls whittled from pine or maple by patient fathers and brothers, most of them stiff and clumsy, a few with arms and legs that moved on pegged joints, or more cuddly rag dolls sewed and stuffed by busy mothers from scraps of homespun. Few children had ever seen any other doll. Occasionally a wealthy Boston child boasted a castoff fashion doll, imported from Paris, with outdated dresses of a style that Boston ladies no longer cared to copy. But these dolls were adult and aloof, clearly not made for loving."

Elizabeth George Speare, *Child Life in New England, 1790–1840.* Sturbridge, Mass.: Old Sturbridge Village, 1961, pp. 20–21.

7. Jean Gabus, "Aesthetic Principles and General Planning of Educational Exhibitions," in *Museum*, a quarterly published by UNESCO. Vol. 18, no. 1, 1965, p. 2.

8. "To grow up does not mean to outgrow either childhood or adolescence but to make use of them in an adult way. But for the child in us, we should be incapable of intellectual curiosity; but for the adolescent, of serious feeling for other individ-

136

uals. I can imagine a person who had 'outgrown' both, though I have never met one; he would be a completely social official being with no personal identity. All that a mature man can give his child and adolescent in return for what they keep giving him are humility, humour, charity and hope."

W. H. Auden, quoted in *A. E. Housman: A Collection of Critical Essays*, ed. Christopher Ricks. Englewood Cliffs, N.J.: Prentice-Hall, 1968, p.4.

9. A London correspondent to the *New York Times* wrote: "Until I visited the exhibition 'Play Orbit' at the Institute of Contemporary Arts, I should hardly have thought the question worth puzzling over. . . . Suddenly, it becomes important to decide what is a toy. All definitions seem to lead into a paradoxical cul-de-sac. A toy is not necessarily art, yet it is something more than a tool. It imitates and represents the real world but it must be susceptible of being explored, challenged, neglected, bullied, even destroyed, without danger. It is a substitute for which there is no substitute. It exists for its own sake and yet it should be somehow unfinished. It shouldn't be designed to teach, yet it should help you to learn."

Alan Brien, "London: Old Theater Myth, New Toys," *New York Times*, January 12, 1970, p. 22.

10. I was brought up to believe every word printed in a dictionary, and could not resist consulting still another authority, the latest, best-selling *American Heritage Dictionary of the English Language*, published in 1969. I was dismayed by their commonplace and freewheeling (slang) interpretation of doll: "1. A child's toy representing a baby or other human being. 2. A pretty child. 3. *Slang*. An attractive woman of dubious intelligence." Not so. The word as I knew it was used as a term of admiration. One year later, as I was browsing among the paperbacks in a large bookstore, I noticed the paperback edition which was published in 1970 and turned to doll: "1. A figure representing a baby or other human being, used as

a child's toy. 2. *Slang*. An attractive young woman." This was the moment to renounce all dictionaries.

11. Bil Baird, *The Art of the Puppet*. New York: Macmillan Co., 1965, p. 13.

12. Among my favorite books is one by Lesley Gordon, which has unfortunately long been out of print. It contains delightful, discerning praise of children's toys. She writes that "there is yet another important group of dolls that must be included. . . . Puppets or marionettes have sustained an unbroken career from the days of the ancient Greek theatre."

Lesley Gordon, *Peepshow into Paradise*. London: George G. Harrap & Co., 1953, p. 112.

13. Ralph C. Altman, "Primitive Puppetry," in *History of Puppetry*, exhibition catalogue, Los Angeles County Museum, 1959, p. 5.

14. "In the seventeenth and eighteenth centuries, and earlier still for that matter, the word *toy* meant not only a plaything but also a trifle, a small article of little intrinsic value. Thus such items as buttons, cheap jewelry, and odds and ends that today one might buy at a notions counter in an American store could be classed as toys, as could pottery ornaments, money boxes, and the knicknacks and gewgaws sold at fairs and now collected under the category of *fairings*."

Ivor Noël Hume, *A Guide to Artifacts of Colonial America*. New York: Alfred A. Knopf, 1970, p. 313.

15. "Dolls are not, as has been assumed all too readily, age-old archetypal playthings. . . . Nothing could be further from the facts. What are regarded unequivocally as dolls representing ancient cultures were simply objects of ritualistic and sacred import."

Leslie Daiken, *Children's Toys Throughout the Ages*. New York: Frederick A. Praeger, 1953, p. 102.

16. "Oh sir get the doll a roofing." Re-

ported as the dying words of Arthur Flegenheimer, alias "Dutch Schultz," as transcribed by the Newark Police Department after "Dutch" was shot in a Newark bar in 1935. *Parodies: An Anthology from Chaucer to Beerbohm—and After*, ed. Dwight MacDonald. New York: Random House, 1960, p. 211.

17. *Through the Looking-Glass*, in *The Complete Works of Lewis Carroll*. New York: Modern Library, n.d., p. 214.

18. William Empson, *Seven Types of Ambiguity*. London: Chatto & Windus, 1947, p. viii.

19. Alfonso A. Narvaez, "Where Religion and Superstition Mix in the City," *New York Times*, September 15, 1969, p. 49.

20. "Among the Oloh Ngadju of Borneo, when a sick man is supposed to be suffering from the assaults of a ghost, puppets of dough or rice-meal are made and thrown under the house as substitutes for the patient, who thus rids himself of the ghost. Similarly in the island of Dama, between New Guinea and Celebes, where sickness is ascribed to the agency of demons, the doctor makes a doll of palm-leaf and lays it, together with some betel, rice, and half of an empty eggshell, on the patient's head. Lured by this bait the demon quits the sufferer's body and enters the palm-leaf doll, which the wily doctor thereupon promptly decapitates."

James George Frazer, *The New Golden Bough*, ed. Dr. Theodor H. Gaster. New York: Mentor Books, 1964, p. 539.

21. Avon Neal, *Ephemeral Folk Figures: Scarecrows, Harvest Figures, and Snowmen*. Photographs by Ann Parker. New York: Clarkson N. Potter, 1969, pp. 11–12.

22. "In the gardens of some Tuscan town, against a background of rising hills, some morning in spring under a pale sky, a statue should be erected to Collodi. It would show the artist in the act of carving his famous puppet out of wood. . . . What

am I saying? Another statue? Heaven forbid, there are too many already and they are too ugly. We should instead celebrate very simply every April Pinocchio's anniversary. There would be no speech. There would be dances and songs; there would be a marionette show, games of every kind, and lots of candy, cakes and sweet drinks; and liberty and gaiety and even joy."

Paul Hazard, *Books, Children and Men*, trans. Marguerite Mitchell. Boston: Horn Book, 1960, pp. 118–19.

23. "I came into the W.I. [Women's Institute] movement after I had heard how much the women enjoyed hearing about the old country crafts—they are very keen on the Museum of Rural Life at Stowmarket and nearly everybody treasures some ancient family thing. One of these treasures was a corn-dolly about eighty years old. It was a long plaited tube ending in a bunch of ears and with a handle to hang it up by. An old lady then produced her heirloom corn-dolly which was in the form of Mother Earth and dressed in a long cotton frock and bonnet. It was about two feet high and a hundred years old. It had been passed down in the family and she was going to pass it to her daughter, she said. She said she couldn't give it away because it would be unlucky. About this time I also met a farmer from Framlingham who had to take over a corn-dolly which hung in the kitchen of the farm he had just bought, otherwise his farming would be ruined.

"The dolly was made each harvest, kept until the spring and then 'released' into the newly-sown seed. A woman of about sixty told me that she could remember her grandfather making them. She could recall him plaiting as he ate his bait at harvest-time. She brought one of his dollies along; it was a kind of goddess and she had wrapped it in a plastic bag. The origins of the dollies are very vague and go right back to the ancient Egyptians and Greeks. They were made because people were scared of extinction. They could have been a gift of appeasement to the gods or a way of preserving the spirit of the corn. They were made in the shape of Ceres or a horn of plenty, or just a corn cage to keep the fertility symbol in until the next sowing. But eventually people made them into the shapes of things belonging to a certain part of the country. In Essex the dolly is made like a terret which can be worn on a horse collar and the Suffolk emblem is a horseshoe because of the Suffolk Punch and because this was the land of the great horsemen. The Cambridgeshire bell-dolly came from the practice of ringing bells when the last load of corn was brought in off the fields. They have a lantern in Norfolk which they think originated from Rumania. The Roman legions who were stationed in Norfolk came from Rumania and it is believed that they brought their harvest-dolly with them.

"Hardly anybody could remember them before I talked about them. Now they are very keen to learn how to make them. Although, when I told the W.I. that they could be turned into attractive decorations for harvest festival an old lady jumped up and cried, 'How dare you think of putting a pagan idol in our church!' "

Ronald Blythe, *Akenfield: Portrait of an English Village*. New York: Pantheon Books, 1969, pp. 204–5.

24. The rich, beautiful prose style of a mail-order catalogue offers a number of surprises. One of the best entries is: "EEYOW! 'LIVING' MONSTER SCARES YOU— DROPS HIS PANTS & BLUSHES! To panic your friends, push the button on electronic Frankenstein. He groans and jerks both arms to attack when his trousers suddenly drop and he actually blushes in embarrassment. Party guests will clamor for repeat performances. Terrorific metal and rubber monster has cloth garments."

25. "As for uniqueness or rarity we are agreed, I am sure, that however important those qualities may be to the collector of postage stamps, rarity makes a work of art no whit more desirable to the patron or enjoyer. I should go further and say on the other hand that, though commonness contains no element of beauty or of non-beauty, commonness of good things is so desirable that some conscientious citizens spend their lives trying to make beautiful and useful things available to rich and poor alike."

Langdon Warner, *The Enduring Art of Japan*. Cambridge, Mass.: Harvard University Press, 1952, p. 78.

26. See Aline B. Saarinen, *The Proud Possessors*. New York: Random House, 1958.

27. A great surprise, because it was so unexpected, was finding the joys of doll collecting in *The Locked Room Reader* (ed. Hans' Santesson. New York: Random House, 1968, p. 20), an unlikely source except that it included a masterful tale by Ellery Queen—"The Dauphin's Doll." "In the beginning they were dolls of common clay: a Billiken, a kewpie, a Käthe Kruse, a Patsy, a Foxy Grandpa, and so forth. But then, as her need increased, Miss Ypson began her fierce sack of the past. Down into the land of Pharaoh she went for two pieces of thin desiccated board, carved and painted and with hair of strung beads, and legless— so that they might not run away—which any connoisseur will tell you are the most superb specimens of ancient Egyptian paddle doll extant, far superior to those in the British Museum, although this fact will be denied in certain quarters."

What was denied in "certain quarters" was stated in the Brooklyn Institute of Arts and Sciences *Museum Journal* (1943–44, p. 9) in an article, "Doll, Queen or Goddess?" by Elizabeth Riefstahl: "Before proceeding further, it may be well to demolish thoroughly the theory that our bronzes are dolls. Indeed, of the many ancient Egyptian figurines that have been so classified, I know of not one that I would accept as such without reservation. It is quite possible that little girls played with dolls in Ancient Egypt, but it is more than probable that, from the paddle-shaped wooden 'dolls' of the Middle Kingdom . . . on down to the terra cottas of Roman times, none of the female figurines found in Egypt were dolls in our sense of the word." But they were, in my sense of the word.

28. Walter Benjamin, *Illuminations*, ed. and with an introduction by Hannah

Arendt. New York: Harcourt, Brace & World, 1968, pp. 60–61.

29. "The best known and most numerous Ashanti carvings are the so-called fertility dolls. They could be carried by any pregnant woman to insure the health and beauty of the child. The high forehead symbolized ideal beauty; the ringed neck, health and well-being. . . . The Fanti live on the coast to the south of the Ashanti. Their version of the *Akua'ba* is distinguished by a high rectangular head form."

Roy Sieber and Arnold Rubin, *Sculpture of Black Africa: The Paul Tishman Collection.* Los Angeles County Museum of Art, 1968, pp. 60, 64.

30. Movies have come a long way(?) in exchanging the ignorance of the child for the befuddlement of today's parent; in a *Punch* cartoon by J. W. Taylor, the mother asks her daughter: "Which is the goodie, dear—the infanticide or the procuress?"

31. *The Golem* was the fifth major German film to be shown in this country after the end of World War I. It opened at a small New York theater on June 19, 1921.

32. "The Golem's fame in the West is owed to the work of the Austrian writer Gustav Meyrink, who in the fifth chapter of his dream novel *Der Golem* (1915) writes:

'It is said that the origin of the story goes back to the seventeenth century. According to lost formulas of the Kabbalah, a rabbi [Judah Loew ben Bezabel] made an artificial man—the aforesaid Golem—so that he would ring the bells and take over all the menial tasks of the synagogue.

'He was not a man exactly, and had only a sort of dim, half-conscious, vegetative existence. By the power of a magic tablet which was placed under his tongue and which attracted the free sidereal energies of the universe, this existence lasted during the daylight hours.

'One night before evening prayer, the rabbi forgot to take the tablet out of the Golem's mouth, and the creature fell into a frenzy, running out into the dark alleys of the ghetto and knocking down those who got in his way, until the rabbi caught up with him and removed the tablet. At once the creature fell lifeless. All that was left of him is the dwarfish clay figure that may be seen today in the New Synagogue.' "

Jorge Luis Borges with Margarita Guerrero, *The Book of Imaginary Beings*, rev., enl., and trans. in collaboration with the author by Norman Thomas di Giovanni. New York: E. P. Dutton & Co., 1969, pp. 113–14.

33. Charles Dickens, *Martin Chuzzlewit.* London: J. M. Dent & Sons, 1957, p. 303.

34. "But one thing should be noted: the phenomenon of collecting loses its meaning as it loses its personal owner. Even though public collections may be less objectionable socially and more useful academically than private collections, the objects get their due only in the latter. . . . As Hegel put it, only when it is dark does the owl of Minerva begin its flight. Only in extinction is the collector comprehended."

Walter Benjamin, *op. cit.*, p. 67.

35. Dorothy S., Elizabeth A., and Evelyn J. Coleman, *The Collector's Encyclopedia of Dolls.* New York: Crown Publishers, 1968, p. 450.

Special homage must be paid to the indefatigable Colemans, whose *Encyclopedia* is, of all the books read, glanced at, or thumbed through, the one which is alone indispensable if you would know the history and manufacture of the doll in Europe and the United States. I have referred to it when in doubt, when I needed additional facts, when I was curious as to who made what doll, how, when, and where. It is a monumental achievement of research and dedication to the world of dolls within the Colemans' self-avowed "limited definition." Discovering the sheer number of manufactured dolls (through 1925) is a humbling experience, much like reading the obituary pages of all newspapers in all languages over the centuries. How many billions of dolls have been made, sold, dressed, and lost is beyond our comprehension.

36. Mary Hillier, *Dolls and Doll-Makers.* New York: G. P. Putnam's Sons, 1968, p. 136.

37. John Noble, *Dolls.* New York: Walker and Co., 1967, p. 71.

38. Quoted in Janet Pagter Johl, *Your Dolls and Mine: A Collectors' Handbook.* New York: H. L. Lindquist, 1952, pp. 37–38.

39. Quoted in Mary Hillier, *op. cit.*, p. 235.

40. Quoted in Evelyn, Elizabeth, and Dorothy Coleman, *The Age of Dolls.* Washington, D.C.: Dorothy S. Coleman, 1965, pp. 63–64.

41. Max von Boehn, *Dolls and Puppets*, trans. Josephine Nicoll, with a note on puppets by George Bernard Shaw, rev. ed. Boston: Charles T. Branford Co., 1956, pp. 134–36.

42. Coleman, *The Collector's Encyclopedia of Dolls, op. cit.*, p. 224.

43. Ibid., p. 224.

44. Ibid., p. 239

45. Quoted in Alfred Chapuis and Edmond Droz, *Automata: A Historical and Technological Study*, trans. Alec Reid. Neuchâtel, Switzerland: Éditions du Griffon, 1958, p. 14.

46. Ibid., p. 15.

47. Ibid., p. 15.

48. Ibid., p. 315.

49. Coleman, *The Collector's Encyclopedia of Dolls, op. cit.*, p. 507.

50. Ibid.

51. "The toys of 100 years ago still have power to enchant us with their ingenuity, their humour, their taste—in a word, their charm. Nothing better has been made since, nor, in this plastic mass-production age, is it likely to be. . . . The catch-phrase changes from year to year, but the plain fact remains that the major-

ity of toys are designed and made by grown-ups to appeal—that is, to sell—to other adults. Children merely provide an excuse."

Jac Remise and Jean Fondin, *The Golden Age of Toys*, English text by D. B. Tubbs. Lausanne, Switzerland: Edita Lausanne, 1967, pp. 11, 14.

52. Coleman, *The Collector's Encyclopedia of Dolls*, op. cit.

53. David Manning White and Robert H. Abel, eds., *The Funnies: An American Idiom*. New York: Free Press of Glencoe, 1963, p. 22.

54. " 'Spaces' [an exhibition at the Museum of Modern Art] attempts to spot a new trend in art—one that moves away from the production of 'collectible' objects engaging the viewer only visually, toward the use of 'real' space that calls into play his entire perceptual equipment. 'This art doesn't give you very much of a handle,' says Jennifer Licht, associate curator of painting and sculpture at the museum, who organized the show. 'It doesn't offer you a finite object, but a set of conditions. The artists here are not isolating visual perception, but going into a larger, more encompassing art, whose interior space you can enter into and perceive with your body.' "

Grace Glueck, "Museum Beckoning Space Explorers," *New York Times*, January 2, 1970, p. 34.

55. "Sexless, like children's dolls."

Rainer Maria Rilke, "Puppen," *Five Prose Pieces*, trans. Carl Niemeyer. Cummington, Mass.: Cummington Press, 1947, p. 16.

56. A Citizens Committee to Protest Little Brother Doll was formed by a group of mothers in Ohio. "The Committee's first act was to send a letter protesting Little Brother to 'elected officials, churches, clubs, organizations and citizens' urging them to take a firm stand against the doll. [They wrote:] 'Toys are, should be, and must remain objects of play. Sex organs are not. There must be

no part on a toy that a mother reprimands her child that it is not nice to play with. A simple "What's that?" asked by a 2-, 3- or 4-year-old must not force us into a vocabulary or subject matter beyond the realm of their understanding.' "

Barbara W. Wyden, "Little Brother Comes to America," *New York Times Magazine*, October 29, 1967, p. 79.

57. "The Refaberts were aware that such a doll, if it were to be put on the market, must be physically and artistically impeccable. Mrs. Refabert sought a prototype in the sculptures at Chartres, in the paintings of Rubens and Raphael. She visited the Alte Pinakothek in Munich and searched through the chapels and palazzos of Rome. Finally, in Florence, she found her model, the disarming cherub with a dolphin, the Verrocchio statue in the Palazzo Vecchio. . . . A mold was made and submitted to the august Institut Pédagogique de France, a branch of the Ministry of Education. The Institut pondered and finally declared that Little Brother was a 'very nice idea,' but that it would prefer to see him modeled as 'a real baby, not as an angel.' Mrs. Refabert produced another mold and another and another. Her sixth effort won approval." Ibid., p. 77.

58. Ernest Leogrande, "Decisions, Decisions: Now It's the Doll That Has Everything," *New York Sunday News*, May 28, 1967.

59. Ralph Ellison, *The Invisible Man*. New York: Random House, 1947, p. 7.
60. Rag doll, Newark Museum, about 1870.

61. Knitted doll, Essex Institute, Salem, Mass., about 1892.

62. "The *kachinas* . . . are the invisible forces of life—not gods, but rather intermediaries, messengers. Hence their chief function is to bring rain, insuring the abundance of crops and the continuation of life. . . . Dr. J. W. Fewkes, in his classic first study of Hopi *kachinas* a half-century ago, identified about 220. Estimates by

later statistical anthropologists range up to 335. This enumeration of *kachinas* is akin to measuring how many angels can be accommodated on the head of a pin."

Frank Waters, *Book of the Hopi*. New York: Ballantine Books, 1969, pp. 202, 205.

63. Ibid., p. 205.

64. Ibid., p. 26. "Zuñi is the only other pueblo which has *kachinas*; these, say the Hopis, were given by the Hopis who preceded them during the Emergence" (pp. 205–6).

65. " 'Art' and 'society' are two of the vaguest concepts in modern language. . . . In the English language the word 'art' is so ambiguous that no two people will spontaneously define it in the same sense. Sophisticated people will try to isolate some characteristic common to all the arts—they then find themselves involved in the science of art, in aesthetics, finally in metaphysics. Simple people tend to identify art with one of the arts, usually painting. They are confused if they are asked to consider music or architecture as art. Common to both sophisticated and simple people is the assumption that whatever art may be, it is a specialist or professional activity of no direct concern to the average man."

Sir Herbert Read, "The Necessity of Art," in *The Arts and Man*, op. cit., p. 27.

66. "We do not know when the carving of kachinas, an art still vital to the Pueblo people, was initiated but it is probably of fairly recent origin. The earliest dated carvings go back to 1869."

George Mills, *Kachinas and Saints: A Contrast in Style and Culture*. Colorado Springs: Taylor Museum, Fine Arts Center, n.d.

67. "Art with the Indian had a strong psychological value, as it does with all people. Not all of it had religious or ceremonial content; much was simply to please the user."

Frederick J. Dockstader, *Indian Art in*

America. Greenwich, Conn.: New York Graphic Society, n.d., p. 45.

68. "All children talk to their toys; toys become actors in the great drama of life, which is reduced to the measure of the camera obscura of their little brains. Children demonstrate through their games their great talent for abstraction and their enormous imaginative power.... This facility with which children satisfy their imagination is a token of the spirituality of their artistic concepts. The toy is the child's initiation into art, or rather it is his initiation into its practical application, and when he has come to man's estate no perfect work of art will ever arouse in him the same warmth, or the same enthusiasm, or the same confidence."

Charles Baudelaire, "Morale du joujou," from *Le Monde Littéraire,* 1853, trans. Barbara Wright in *Play Orbit,* ed. Jasia Reichardt. London: Studio International, 1969, p. 14.

69. Charlotte Brontë, *Jane Eyre.* Cleveland and New York: World, 1946, p. 35.

70. The following is from a letter written to me in 1967 by Mrs. Johnie Head, Arkansas: "I have made dolls for about 33 years, raised our children, keeping house, making a garden, raising chickens, milking cows, raising rabbits, canning vegetables and fruits and berries. Raised 6 children. My husband and I lived on a big farm. He made the crops and took care of the hay. In between work at home and after the crops were laid by he bailed hay for other people with an old time horse bailer. We really had to work hard. I made and sold dolls. Made them mostly at night. I am a widow now. I don't think anyone else makes the dolls like I do for I just studied these dolls and how to make them myself. No one elses ideas or patterns to go by. Strictly worked out with my own mind and hands. I don't think anyone else makes the horses or cows now. All of my cornshuck dolls are characters of people I can remember when I

was 5 years old from 1906 on up through my childhood. I make a group like mother milking and baby and little sister watching, and Grandma Beckie smoking, waiting for a meal of corn bread and butter and sorghum molasses which used to be a very common meal when I was small on the farm. The children all went to church in those days. Anyway, it's a true story, a story made up into dolls. I make Uncle Nate and plow with a white mule. Grandpa Farley sledding. Grandpa Randy carding, Grandma Amanda spinning, Mom making lye soap. Grandma Beckie churning and Grandpa smoking. Ozark ranch rider on horse Speck. Woman riding side saddle with children. The unwanted mother who was thrown out. Ozark farmers quartet with piano, these are like the real quartets my husband was part of."

71. "I'm afraid I don't understand anything more at all ... even the simplest things have got in a muddle. Is it 'I' who draw the bow, or is it the bow that draws me into the state of highest tension? Do 'I' hit the goal, or does the goal hit me? ... Bow, arrow, goal and ego, all melt into one another, so that I can no longer separate them. And even the need to separate has gone. For as soon as I take the bow and shoot, everything becomes so clear and straightforward and so ridiculously simple."

Eugen Herrigel, *Zen in the Art of Archery.* New York: Pantheon, 1953, p. 88.

72. Maisy M. Coburn, *Handcrafted Apple Face Dolls.* Quitman, Arkansas, n.d., p. 7.

73. "He knows that the innermost core of every one demands an immediate satisfaction, in the spoon no less than in the food, in the instrument as well as in the music. He is not waiting, as so many others are, till wars shall have been averted, revolutions made, or inventions perfected, before he begins to fashion the

world nearer to the heart's desire. Each in his own very small way is doing it now. The craftsman is preserving a truth indispensable to the future of mankind."

Seonaid Mairi Robertson, *Craft and Contemporary Culture.* London: George G. Harrap & Co. and UNESCO, 1961, p. 30.

74. Henry Mayhew, *Mayhew's London, Being Selections from 'London Labour and the London Poor,'* which was first published in 1851, ed. Peter Quennell, London: Spring Books, n.d., pp. 186–87.

75. "For all art is essentially play—as all full living is a game that is enjoyed. This is probably the basic explanation of those frail or arid reaches which occasionally appear in the history of art: the failure of art in those times to express and to refresh itself in play. When a culture begins to regard play as something not quite respectable that culture is already facing sterility. To keep an art or culture fertile it must be 'played.' "

James Johnson Sweeney, *Miró: Recent Paintings.* New York: Pierre Matisse, 1953.

76. "For several hundred years, in the West, people have been losing something of the right notion of beauty that is ordinary and have largely stopped making common things beautifully. Surely in the past ordinary things have been made in the West by unnamed craftsmen in a manner so beautiful and adequate that no genius could do better. Is it not possible that there is a domain in art where genius has no concern?"

Langdon Warner, *The Enduring Art of Japan, op. cit.,* p. 82.

77. Ruth E. and R. C. Mathes, "The Artifacts of Childhood," *The Museologist,* Rochester Fine Arts Museum, June, 1968.

78. Bettina [Ehrlich], *Dolls.* London: Oxford University Press, 1962.

SELECTED BIBLIOGRAPHY

Beier, H. U. *The Story of Sacred Wood Carvings from One Small Yoruba Town*. Lagos, Nigeria: Nigeria Magazine, 1957.

Boehn, Max von. *Dolls and Puppets*. Translated by Josephine Nicoll. Newton Centre, Mass.: Charles T. Branford, rev. ed. 1956.

Brenda [Mrs. Castle Smith]. "Victoria-Bess: The Ups and Downs of a Doll's Life." In *Victorian Doll Stories*, ed. Gillian Elise Avery. New York: Schocken Books, 1969.

Caillois, Roger. *Man, Play, and Games*. Translated by Meyer Barash. New York: Free Press of Glencoe, 1961.

Caudill, Harry M. *Night Comes to the Cumberlands*. Boston: Little, Brown, 1963.

Chapuis, Alfred, and Droz, Edmond. *Automata: A Historical and Technological Study*. Translated by Alec Reid. Neuchâtel: Éditions du Griffon, 1958.

Chinese Medicine: An Exhibition Illustrating the Traditional System of Medicine of the Chinese People. London: The Wellcome Historical Medical Museum and Library, 1966.

Christensen, Erwin O. *Early American Wood Carving*. Cleveland: World, 1952.

———. *The Index of American Design*. New York: Macmillan, 1950.

Coburn, Maisy M. *Handcrafted Apple Face Dolls*. Quitman, Ark.: no publisher, n. d.

Cole, Adeline P. *Notes on the Collection of Dolls and Figurines at the Wenham Museum*. Salem, Mass.: Wenham Historical Association, 1951.

Coleman, Dorothy S., Elizabeth A., and Evelyn J. *The Collector's Encyclopedia of Dolls*. New York: Crown, 1968.

Coleman, Elizabeth Ann. "Nineteenth and Twentieth Century Dolls and Their Manufacture." *The Museum* (Newark), Summer, 1968, pp. 1–22.

Coleman, Evelyn, Elizabeth, and Dorothy. *The Age of Dolls*. Washington, D.C.: Dorothy S. Coleman, 1965.

Colton, Harold S. *Hopi Kachina Dolls*. Albuquerque: University of New Mexico Press, 1964.

Cordwell, Justine M. "African Art." In *Continuity and Change in African Cultures*, eds. William R. Bascom and Melville J. Herskovits. Chicago: University of Chicago Press, Phoenix Books, 1962.

Counts, Charles. *Encouraging American Handcrafts*. Washington, D.C.: U.S. Department of Commerce, 1966.

Creekmore, Betsey B. *Traditional American Crafts*. New York: Hearthside Press, 1968.

Culff, Robert. *The World of Toys*. London: Paul Hamlyn, 1969.

Culin, Stewart. *Games of the Orient: Korea, China, Japan*. Rutland, Vt.: Charles E. Tuttle, 1958.

Daiken, Leslie. *World of Toys*. Sidcup, England: Lambarde Press, 1963.

De la Mare, Walter. *Come Hither: A Collection of Rhymes and Poems for the Young of All Ages*. New York: Alfred A. Knopf, 1960.

Dockstader, Frederick J. *The Kachina and the White Man*. Bloomfield Hills, Mich.: Cranbrook Institute of Science, 1954.

DuPuy, Edward L. *Artisans of the Appalachians*. Text by Emma Weaver. Asheville, N. C.: Miller Print Co., 1967.

Dutton, Bertha P. *Indian Artistry in Wood and Other Media*. Santa Fe: Museum of New Mexico Press, 1957.

Early, Alice K. *English Dolls, Effigies and Puppets*. London: B. T. Batsford, 1955.

Eaton, Allen. *Handicrafts of the Southern Highlands*. New York: Russell Sage Foundation, 1937.

Fagg, William. *Nigerian Images*. New York: Frederick A. Praeger, 1963.

Fawcett, Clara Hallard. *Dolls: A New Guide for Collectors*. Newton Centre, Mass.: Charles T. Branford, 1964.

Fewkes, J. Walter. *Hopi Kachinas*. Twenty-first Annual Report of the Bureau of American Ethnology. Washington, D. C.: Smithsonian Institution, 1903.

Foley, Daniel. *Toys Through the Ages*. Philadelphia: Chilton Books, 1962.

Fraser, Antonia. *A History of Toys*. New York: Delacorte Press, 1966.

Freeman, Ruth. *Encyclopedia of American Dolls*. Watkins Glen, N.Y.: Century House, 1952.

Freeman, Ruth and Larry. *Cavalcade of Toys*. Watkins Glen, N.Y.: Century House, 1942.

Fritzsch, Karl Ewald, and Bachmann, Manfred. *An Illustrated History of Toys*. Translated by Ruth Michaelis-Jena. London: Abbey Library, 1966.

Girard, Alexander. *The Magic of a People*. New York: Viking Press, 1968.

Gordon, Lesley. *A Pageant of Dolls*. New York: A. A. Wyn, 1949.

———. *Peepshow into Paradise*. London: George G. Harrap, 1953.

Griffith, James S. *Legacy of Conquest: The Arts of Northwest Mexico*. Colorado Springs: Fine Arts Center,

Taylor Museum, 1967.

Hansen, H. J., ed. *European Folk Art*. New York: Mc-Graw-Hill, 1968.

Hercík, Emanuel. *Folktoys, les jouets populaires*. Prague: Orbis, 2nd ed. 1952.

Hertz, Louis H. *The Toy Collector*. New York: Funk & Wagnalls, 1969.

Hillier, Mary. *Dolls and Doll-Makers*. New York: G. P. Putnam's Sons, 1968.

Holme, C. Geoffrey, ed. *Children's Toys of Yesterday*. London: The Studio, 1932.

Huizinga, Johan. *Homo Ludens: A Study of the Play-Element in Culture*. Boston: Beacon Press, 1955.

Jackson, Mrs. F. Nevill. *Toys of Other Days*. New York: Benjamin Blom, 1968.

Jacobs, Flora Gill. *A History of Dolls' Houses*. New York: Charles Scribner's Sons, 1965.

Johl, Janet Pagter. *Your Dolls and Mine: A Collectors' Handbook*. New York: H. L. Lindquist, 1952.

Kainen, Ruth Cole. *America's Christmas Heritage*. New York: Funk & Wagnalls, 1969.

Kramrisch, Stella. *Unknown India: Ritual Art in Tribe and Village*. Philadelphia: Museum of Art, 1968.

Kyle, Thomas. *People Figures*. New York: Museum of Contemporary Crafts, 1966.

Laliberte, Norman, and Jones, Maureen. *Wooden Images*. New York: Van Nostrand-Reinhold Books, 1966.

Larkin, Oliver W. *Art and Life in America*. New York: Rinehart, new ed. 1956.

Larrabee, Eric, ed. *Museums and Education*. Washington, D.C.: Smithsonian Institution, 1968.

Latham, Jean. *Dolls' Houses: A Personal Choice*. New York: Charles Scribner's Sons, 1969.

Leuzinger, Elsy. *Africa: The Art of the Negro Peoples*. New York: McGraw-Hill, 1960.

Lewis, Arthur. *Hex*. New York: Trident Press, 1969.

McClintock, Inez and Marshall. *Toys in America*. Washington, D.C.: Public Affairs Press, 1961.

Mathes, Ruth E. and R. C. "The Artifacts of Childhood." *The Museologist*, Rochester Fine Arts Museum, June, 1968.

————. "The Decline and Fall of the Wooden Doll," *Doll Collectors Manual*, 1964.

Mills, George. *Kachinas and Saints: A Contrast in Style and Culture*. Colorado Springs: Fine Arts Center, Taylor Museum, n. d.

Montessori, Maria. *The Child in the Family*. Chicago:

Henry Regnery, 1970.

Murray, Patrick. *Toys*. London: Studio Vista, 1968.

Noble, John. *Dolls*. New York: Walker, 1967.

Plass, Margaret. *African Tribal Sculpture*. Philadelphia: University Museum, 1956.

Riefstahl, Elizabeth. "Doll, Queen or Goddess?" *Museum Journal*, Brooklyn Institute of Arts and Sciences, no. 2, 1943–44, pp. 7–21.

Rijksmuseum, Amsterdam. *Dolls' Houses*. Introduction by J. H. M. Leesberg-Terwindt. 1967.

St. George, Eleanor. *Dolls of Three Centuries*. New York: Charles Scribner's Sons, 1951.

————. *The Dolls of Yesterday*. New York: Charles Scribner's Sons, 1948.

Shishido, Misako. *The Folk Toys of Japan*. Tokyo: Japan Publications, 1963.

Sieber, Roy, and Rubin, Arnold. *Sculpture of Black Africa: The Paul Tishman Collection*. Los Angeles County Museum of Art, 1968.

Slivka, Rose. "The American Craftsman 1964," *Craft Horizons* 24, May, 1964, pp. 10–11.

Speaight, George. *Juvenile Drama: The History of the English Toy Theatre*. London: Macdonald, 1946.

Speare, Elizabeth George. *Child Life in New England, 1790–1840*. Sturbridge, Mass.: Old Sturbridge Village, 1961.

Stone, Wilbur Macey. *A Showing of Paper Dolls and Other Cut-Out Toys*. Newark: The Newark Museum, 1931.

Taylor, Francis Henry. *The Taste of Angels*. Boston: Little, Brown, 1948.

Toor, Francis. *A Treasury of Mexican Folkways*. New York: Crown, 1962.

Trowell, Margaret. *Classical African Sculpture*. New York: Frederick A. Praeger, 1964.

Victoria and Albert Museum. *Dolls*. London: Her Majesty's Stationery Office, 1960.

White, Gwen. *Dolls of the World*. Newton Centre, Mass.: Charles T. Branford, 1963.

Working Committee on Good Toys. *Good Toys: A Short Guide*. Ravensburg: Otto Maier Verlag, 1960.

Yamada, Tokubee. *Japanese Dolls*. Tokyo: Japan Travel Bureau, 2nd ed. 1959.

Yanagi, Sôetsu. *Folk-Crafts in Japan*. Tokyo: Kokusai Bunka Shinkokai (Society for International Cultural Relations), 1936.